This Special Edition of Latex Mask Making: A Workshop with Russ Adams is dedicated to my dear friends at INIFICON and ALL CON. I have been so incredibly grateful for the years I have spent with the staff and the fans of these amazing organizations. I am honored to have been your guest and your friend.

Latex Mask Making

A Workshop with Russ Adams

Latex Mask Making: A Workshop with Russ Adams ©2017 by Russ Adams. All rights reserved, including the right to reproduce this book or portions thereof in any form without the express permission of the publisher.

Photographs, layout, design, and illustrations: Russ Adams

Copy edited by Jan Hamer
Content edited by Dr. Victoria Ramirez
Published in the United States of America by Old Scottish Bastard Media, LLC
1501 W 2650 S STE 105
Ogden UT, 84401

ISBN-13:978-1548840310
ISBN-10:1548840319

Russ Adams websites
Author Page: www.russadams.me
Professional Page: www.escapedesignfx.com

By the Same Author

A BIT ABOUT THE AUTHOR

I am well-known special effects artist. I own a studio called Escape Design FX in Utah. I have also worked in the industry for nearly 20 years. My work has been seen in countless films, on television, and commercials. In fact, I travel the world teaching puppet creation, makeup effects, and mask making. As you probably noticed, I am also an author with a series of how-to books called A Workshop with Russ Adams.

Author Site: (http://www.russadams.me)

Escape Design FX: (http://www.escapedesignfx.com)

People love my masks and creature suits. They liken my work to wearable works of art, which I greatly appreciate. I try to build things that look just as good on display as they do on a person's body. My masks range from simple eye covers to enormous Torso Masks ™ and creature suits. What I love most about mask making is transforming a human into almost anything I can think of.

As a kid, I was never really impressed with what I found at big box stores or over-produced seasonal offerings. I knew what I wanted and I wasn't going to find it at the local shopping mall. I started to make my own stuff very early on, first out of necessity. My family didn't have a ton of money, so if I wanted something the most likely way of getting it was to build it myself. It's not surprising that I would eventually work in a field where making things from nothing is the name of the game. I started selling my own line of masks after I founded Escape Design FX. And I have been having a blast ever since.

For you, it all starts here. Now, I'd like to share what I've learned with you.

In this book, you will find detailed, step-by-step instructions on how to create your very own latex masks. I've included a list of all the materials you'll need at the beginning of each section. I have also added a checklist at the end of the book as a quick reference guide when you start molding your sculpture. Between the contents of the book and that checklist, you have all the tools to produce a killer latex mask and mold to make as many copies as you like.

Let's get started!

Table of Contents

PREFACE 1

A NOTE ON SAFETY 3

INTRODUCTION 5

COMMON FEARS 7

STEP 1: MAKING THE ARMATURE 9

    Buyer Beware! 10

    Build Your Own 12

    OPTION 1: Styrofoam 12

    Materials 12

    Tools 12

    OPTION 2: The Pipe 19

    Materials 19

    Tools 19

    OPTION 3: Mannequin Option 22

STEP 2: MAKING YOUR SCULPTING TOOLS 23

    Wooden Tools 25

    Materials 25

    Tools 25

    Rake Tools 28

    Materials 28

    Tools 28

    Loop Tools 34

    Materials 34

Tools...	34
Turntable (Lazy Susan)..	36
Materials..	36
Tools...	36
Reference Photos...	43

STEP 3: SCULPTING 45

Materials..	45
Tools...	46
WED Clay...	47
Build Up & Sizing...	50
Blocking...	52
Rough Detail	56
Knocking Down Clay...	57
Fine Detailing	66

STEP 4: THE MOLD 71

Materials..	71
Tools...	71
Sealing the Sculpture	76
Building the Case line..	77
Undercuts	83
Build the Retaining Wall	86
Registrations	88
Sealing..	91
Plaster Layer 1: The First Splash Coat.................................	92
Player Layer 2: The Second Splash Coat	99
Plaster Layer 3: The Insurance Layer	100
Plaster Layer 4: The Protective Layer	104

    Prepping for Side Two 106

    Pry Marks 113

    Building the Second Half of the Mold 116

STEP 5: DEMOLDING **117**

    Materials 117

    Tools 117

    Step 6: Latex Casting 125

    Materials 125

    Tools 125

STEP 7: SEAMING & CLEANING **131**

    Materials 131

    Tools 131

    Seaming 133

    Cleaning 138

STEP 8: FINISHING WORK **141**

    Materials 141

    Tools 141

    Concept 142

    Washes 143

    Fluid Stains 148

    Speckling 150

    Highlights & Shadows 151

    Adornments 154

    Moss 156

WORKSHOP SUMMARY **157**

MOLD MAKING CHECKLIST **161**

Additional Information 163

MANY MORE WORKSHOPS TO COME 165
PROJECT NOTES 166
PROJECT NOTES 167

Latex Mask Making

PREFACE

My goal for this book is to give you the tools to succeed in your latex mask making endeavor by guiding you through a step-by-step process that will increase your odds of success. In this book, you are going to learn more than just how to make a latex mask. I am going to rescue you from the idea that you need to buy specialized tools and equipment to succeed.

In this tutorial, you will learn how to make your own armatures, sculpting tools, and turntables. I am going to show you how to use found items and put them to work for you. I am also going to show you how to recapture and revitalize some materials to make them last you a longer amount of time.

My philosophy is, "Don't buy it, build it." By creating your own tools, you save money—money that could go toward more clay, plaster, or education. A sculpting tool with some other artist's name or studio printed on it isn't going to help you sculpt any better. They are likely poorly made imports marked up to line the pockets of the greedy. So make it, don't buy it. If you must buy it, look at all the options. We will get into this later when we talk about armatures.

When we are done, I hope to have taught you a few things, but I also hope to instill a greater appreciation for the cost and craftsmanship that go into masks made by other independent mask-making artists. When you go to a trade show, artists' markets, or an indie mask designer's website and see their handcrafted work on display, you will have an appreciation for the work because you will have experienced it firsthand.

Russ Adams

Finally, when you order *A Workshop with Russ Adams* you will receive the full lesson from start to finish. For that reason, you may encounter a couple steps which also appear in other books in my series. This is because I wrote each of these books as a stand-alone or self-contained workshop—unlike most special effects tutorials that drag a project out across two or three books or videos.

In this book, *Latex Mask Making: A Workshop with Russ Adams*, I discuss the latex mask-making process, which includes sculpting, molding, casting, seaming, cleaning, and painting, as well as the tool-making instructions mentioned above. I will not pause in the middle of the process and continue the workshop in another book. While I would like you to order other workshops, I would hope you do so because you trust me and want to learn a new special effects process.

Latex Mask Making

A NOTE ON SAFETY

WARNING

You will be using chemicals to create your latex mask, so please make sure you read the safety instructions that come with those materials, and take all necessary precautions to ensure a safe working environment. I will do my best to remind you, but it's your responsibility to keep yourself and your working environment safe.

While latex really is a fun material to work with, some people are allergic to it. Basically, the symptoms run the gamut from hives, itching skin, maybe a stuffy or runny nose, breathing issues, and even chest tightening and blood pressure issues. Stronger reactions can occur, including asthma-like symptoms or even anaphylactic shock. So please be careful. If you don't know whether you are allergic to latex, don't just dive in. Consult a doctor on the best way to test for this if you suspect it.

Finally, a word about plaster. It seems harmless enough, but when plaster is setting it can heat up to as much as 140 degrees Fahrenheit. If you aren't careful you can easily burn yourself. Breathing plaster dust is no fun for your lungs either, and of course just working with the stuff over time can dry out your skin wherever it touches. Make sure you clean it off thoroughly after each work session—wear gloves, a dust mask or respirator, and use lotion to keep your skin hydrated.

Basically, please be smart about your tools and materials. Do that and everything should be fine.

Russ Adams

Latex Mask Making

INTRODUCTION

I truly enjoy making latex masks. The materials are generally easy to find and they are relatively affordable compared to some of the materials we special-effects and mask artists use. As of the time of this publication, I could pick up a gallon of latex for about forty-five dollars. That amount, if used properly, could yield up to four of five masks—maybe more depending on size and surface space.

Plaster, UtlraCal 30, is generally easy to find. You can purchase it online from mask and art supply houses or from a local foundry supply. The price is around thirty-five to forty dollars for fifty pounds. If you can find a local foundry supply, you can get a hundred pounds at roughly the same price as the fifty pounds you would buy at an art supply store. So, it pays to look around. A one-hundred-pound bag can yield as much five mask molds depending on the size of the molds and your experience level.

The clay is another inexpensive material. The standard is WED clay (aka EM-217). It was developed long ago for Disney. In fact, WED is an acronym for Walt E. Disney. This is a water-based clay with a glycerin additive. It's an amazing material designed for large sculptures. You can find the clay at most ceramics stores, special-effects supply houses, or online. WED generally runs about twenty to twenty-five dollars for a fifty-pound box. Keep that in mind if you order online. Shipping is going to be quite a bit for a box that heavy. Then there is the treatment that package is going to receive by delivery personnel. I am sure you have seen the YouTube videos of delivery service personnel throwing, kicking, dropping, and generally mistreating packages. At any rate, a fifty-pound box of WED Clay goes a long way.

Once you get the mask-making process down, your imagination is the limit to what you can come up with next.

COMMON FEARS

The biggest fear most people face coming into a project like this is the unknown. *Where do I begin? Will I be good at sculpting? Material costs are so expensive; can I even afford them? What if I screw something up?* These are all legitimate concerns and I am going to help you through them.

Where to start is probably the biggest problem most people have. It was for me. I grew up in the 1980s, the golden age of practical effects. There are all kinds of idols out there, and when you are a kid they vacillate between superheroes, actors, and musicians. Mine were special effects artists: Rick Baker, Steve Johnson, Stan Winston, and Dick Smith. These were just a few of the men I looked up to as kid from rural Pennsylvania with delusions of working in the film business.

As a kid, I really wanted to know how they made all those wonderfully disgusting critters. Back then, the "how-to" of practical effects was about as well-guarded as Fort Knox. There were no YouTube tutorials cracking the code on makeup processes. There was no Amazon or Google search to find a how-to book on creature building. You were stuck sifting through geriatric card catalogues and microfiche slides. God I feel old right now.

My school library was a joke. I graduated with like sixty other teens. That should give you reference as to how vast my school library was. I am sure you can imagine the size and scope of the library's Hollywood practical-effects section. I had a consuming hunger to learn and the only thing at my disposal was grainy photos in magazines like *Fangoria* with the occasional shot of a creature in progress.

Russ Adams

I learned by studying those photos like a thief casing a bank. Slowly, over the course of several years and tens of thousands of dollars, I started to figure things out.

You have the benefit of learning in an open-source world. YouTube is full of information to help you get started. There are classes and how-to books to help and easy-to-access search engines to find them. And you have me--a self-taught special-effects artist who learned the hard way and understands that you don't have a ton of money, and that you are worried about doing it right.

Some of you might be concerned about your ability, but don't be. I am going to teach you the steps we professional artists use to sculpt. I am going to slow it down to a comfortable pace and teach you to think about things in a different way. This is going to help you with your first creation and carry through to those that follow. This information will make you a more successful mask maker.

I am also going to teach you how to make your own tools to save you a fortune. You'll learned to make your own armatures, sculpting tools, turntables, and finishing tools. You may choose to purchase these things. That's fine. But you will be given the option to do it yourself and become self-sufficient.

I will be here to help you avoid common beginner mistakes, which will minimize your stress over screwing something up. So, relax. Enjoy the ride.

Latex Mask Making

STEP 1: MAKING THE ARMATURE

Armatures are critical in sculpting. They stabilize, support, give structure to a sculpture, and can save you from using unnecessary quantities of clay. Saving clay means saving money, but just as important...saving weight. WED clay is heavy. There will be enough clay weight used in the sculpting of your mask as it is. If you had a solid mass of clay in the core of your mask sculpture rather than an armature, your sculpture would go from ten to fifteen pounds to fifty or even seventy-five pounds.

You might be thinking *I can handle that*. But at that weight, the sculpture could start to collapse and break under its own weight when you tip it back to mold it. The armature will help spread out the ten to fifteen pounds and stabilize your creation.

Let's begin with the design of your armature. What is it? The armature I am using is a human analog armature. It's a fancy way of saying my armature looks like a human head and shoulders. There doesn't need to be any detail in it. It's just the basic shape.

As I have stated, you can buy your armature or build it yourself. There are pluses and minus to both options, but making it yourself can save you money. When you are starting out, saving all the money you can is very important. I am going to talk about a couple ways to build your own armature. I am also going to talk about the pitfalls of buying it. I am even going to talk about great alternatives to buying an armature, and it wouldn't be from an art supplier.

Buyer Beware!

I just told you, "you can make your own armatures." But you can also buy them. They are pricey. They run anywhere from sixty-five dollars to one-hundred-twenty dollars. At sixty-five dollars, you are going to find a polyurethane foam head that will more than likely fall apart as you demold your sculpture. Polyfoam is a weak material. It's not the greatest option when you are starting out. You are likely to make mistakes when you are demolding, which can destroy your armature. The suction/vacuum caused by the moist clay can force you to put a lot of pressure on the armature as you pry the two mold halves apart. That kind of force can tear a foam armature up.

Those of us who are used to demolding know how to avoid this. Seeing as how this is likely your first time, you want to avoid breaking an expensive tool. You just spent sixty-five

Latex Mask Making

dollars or more on an armature and you may only get to use it once? UNACCEPTABLE!

I suggest you hold off on the purchase and construct your own. Who knows, it might be the only armature you'll ever need.

I make and sell resin armatures with a wood and polyfoam core. I use them to teach my Latex Mask Workshops. There are a lot of students new to mask making in those classes and so I need a strong armature to stand up to the punishment only a newcomer can dole out. Those armatures are one-hundred-twenty dollars plus shipping.

I am not here to pimp out my armatures. The expense is steep and unnecessary at this stage. I strongly suggest you build your own and below are a few suggestions using attainable materials that are easy to work with.

Build Your Own

OPTION 1: Styrofoam

Materials

1. Styrofoam head
2. Styrofoam sheet
3. Wood glue
4. Wood dowel
5. Tape
6. Five Minute Epoxy or Epsilon

Tools

1. Utility Knife
2. Scroll Saw
3. Rasp

Styrofoam is a good place to start. You might be thinking, *he just criticized foam-based armature*...and I did. So why might I be telling you to use Styrofoam to build your armature now? I warned you against buying a sixty-five dollar or more foam armature because it could fall apart on you. You aren't going to be as angry over losing fifteen dollars as you would be over losing sixty-five dollars plus shipping. At least in this case you have prepared yourself for an armature meltdown.

You can get sheets of Styrofoam insulation at your local Home Depot or Lowe's. It's relatively inexpensive, around five dollars for a good size sheet. You will also need to purchase one of those cheap foam mannequin heads. You can get these on Amazon for next to nothing. If that isn't an option, you can pick one up at Michael's or JoAnn Fabrics, but they are going to cost much more at these stores. Once a

Latex Mask Making

retailer slaps the word "craft" on a product the price suddenly jumps to an astronomical amount. That's because there is no truth to the term "starving artist." All artists are independently wealthy. Didn't you know that?

The foam head comes with a neck, so we are going to have to put the shoulders on ourselves. Create a pattern of a large stretched-out oval that looks like it could be a cross section of your shoulders. You are going to trace this out on the sheet of Styrofoam you purchased at Lowe's or Home Depot.

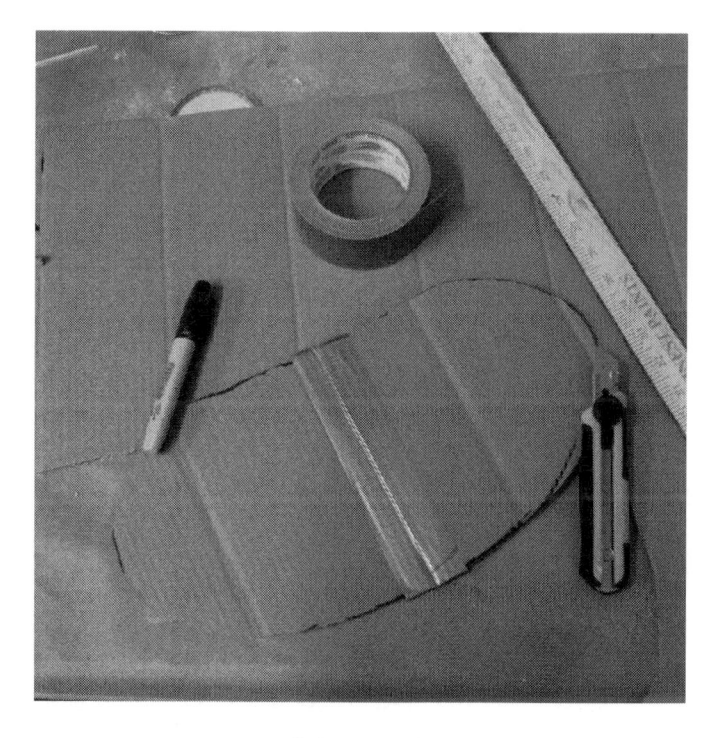

Diagram 1

Once you have traced out the pattern at least three times, start cutting them out. I use a scroll saw to cut these out, but you can use a small hand saw or even a utility knife. BE CAREFUL!

After you have cut the oval shapes out, stack all three on top of each other. Then set the foam head on top. If you like the size of it, we can move on. If not, add another layer of Styrofoam.

> **NOTE:** Don't go too high on this armature. It's a good idea to keep the shoulder height about five to six inches. You don't need a full torso. If the armature is too tall, you may have a problem with your sculpture being top-heavy. Trust me, you don't want to put a ton of work into a sculpture and have it fall over and hit the floor. Bigger isn't always better.

Once you have determined the height you like, you can start gluing the pieces together. You might be tempted to carve some material away from the stack of foam, but don't. We aren't there yet. I typically use wood glue to bond these together. Superglue, spray glue, and hot glue can eat away at the surface of the Styrofoam and destroy your material, so avoid these.

Once you get the layers glued together and the excess glue cleaned up, you can turn your attention to the head.

There is usually a hole in the neck of these Styrofoam heads. I suggest you drive a wooden dowel into the neck hole and then into the Stryofoam sheets. First, determine how far the dowel will go into the neck, then make a mark on the wood as seen in Diagram 2. Then take the measurement off the stack of Styrofoam—add that to the dowel. Cut the dowel.

Latex Mask Making

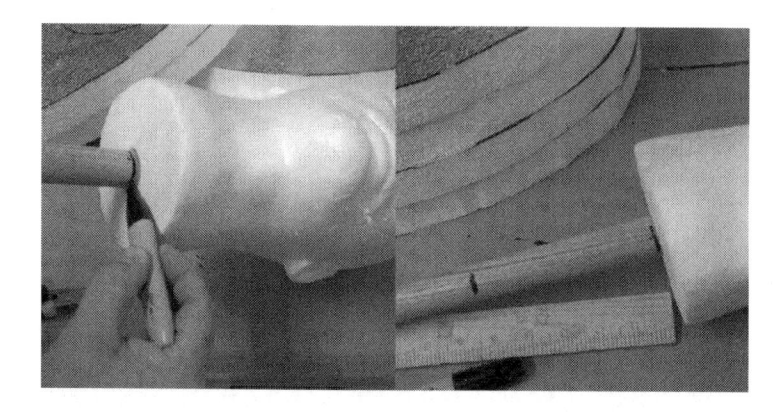

Diagram 2

I would sharpen one end of the dowel to make it easier to insert into the stack of shoulder Styrofoam. Find a good placement to insert the dowel. When you are ready, coat the dowel with wood glue and drive it into the shoulder foam with the sharp end pointed down. Then jam the head on the dowel until the neck contacts the shoulders. See Diagram 3

Russ Adams

Diagram 3

I am going to suggest setting some books on top of the shoulders to prevent the foam from curling up while the glue is drying. Then use some masking tape and tape the head to the shoulders, for the same reason. A good long piece of tape should do the trick. Start at the top of the head and affix the tape to the "chest" and the "back" of your Styrofoam stack. Step away and let the glue dry overnight.

Latex Mask Making

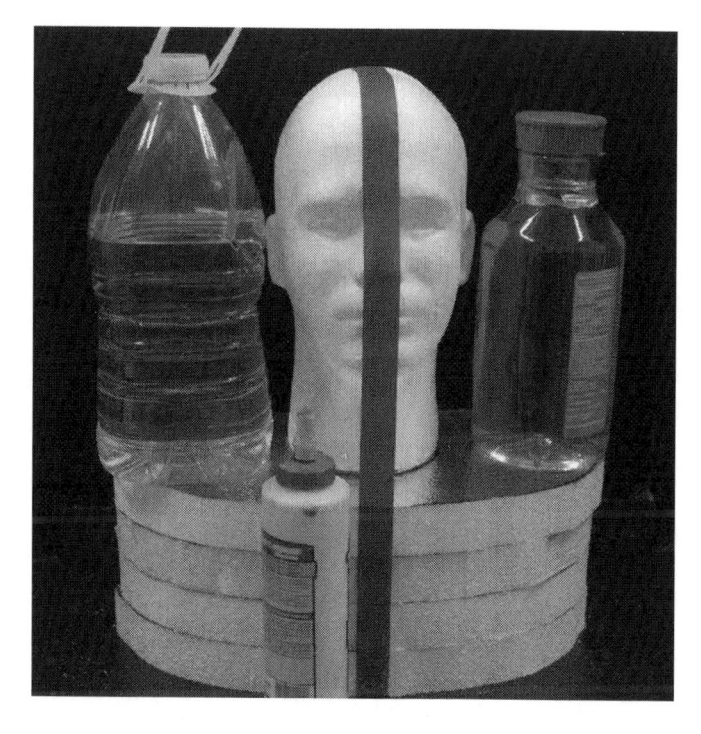

Diagram 4

When the glue is set, remove the tape and books from the armature. You can now use a rasp to smooth and round out the shape of the shoulders and neck area. Once it looks about right, you can use it as is, or coat it with epoxy.

Epoxy won't eat the Styrofoam so it's safe to use. This is not a necessary step, but it will strengthen your armature by creating a protective shell. You will need several layers to give it strength.

When it comes to epoxies, you can use Epsilon, from www.smooth-on.com, which works very well. One of their trial kits will be more than enough to coat your armature. It's

17

a much cheaper route than mixing a bunch of five-minute epoxy.

> **NOTE:** You need to wear a respirator, gloves, and have adequate ventilation when using these epoxies.

Diagram 5

Latex Mask Making

OPTION 2: The Pipe

Materials

1. Plywood
2. Threaded plumbing pipe
3. Flange
4. Screws
5. Aluminum foil

Tools

1. Drill
2. Screwdriver
3. Saw
4. Straight Edge (Ruler or Yardstick)

You can also create a reasonable armature using a sheet of plywood as a base, a piece of plumbing pipe with a threaded end, and a matching flange. A flange is often a round metal disk with a threaded female end in the center. There is a flange in Diagram 7, which is attached to the pipe. This is a more traditional looking armature and adds stability, but to bulk it up you'll be packing it with aluminum foil. It's also a bit more expensive than Option 1, but faster.

Cut the plywood out to about 12"x 12". Once the plywood is cut, you need to find the center. The easiest way of doing this is to grab a straight edge ruler and lay it diagonally across the surface from one corner to the other as shown in Diagram 6.

Diagram 6

Draw a line between these two corners with a marker. Repeat this with the other two corners. The center of the board is where the lines intersect.

Place your flange down on that center mark. Using a drill with a Philips-head bit, screw several drywall screws through the holes on the flange and into the wood. Depending on the length of the screws, you might have some ends poking out on the bottom. If you do, grind them down using a grinder or a Dremel with a stone attachment. In case you don't know what a Dremel is, it's a name-brand rotary tool and can come in handy. You can find other rotary tool options at stores like Harbor Freight, Sears, Home Depot, etc. Again, wear your protective gear…safety glasses and dust mask.

Latex Mask Making

Next, take the threaded pipe, about eight to twelve inches long, and screw it into the flange.

You can wad up and add a lot of aluminum foil to this armature and reduce the amount of clay you need to accomplish your sculpture. Thankfully, aluminum foil is cheap. The downside is a lot of waste. Please recycle it when you are done with the foil.

If you like, you can combine Option 1 and 2 together in various ways.

Diagram 7

OPTION 3: Mannequin Option

If you don't want to build an armature, or buy an expensive piece of garbage, you can use a mannequin. There are several mannequins that you can use, but if this is the route you wish to take, I suggest you buy a mannequin that has a head and basic shoulders. Don't try to use a full mannequin torso on your first mask. You want an armature with shoulders to help stabilize the sculpture. More surface space on the base means more stability.

These types of mannequins are also made of strong plastic or fiberglass, so they can handle the pressure of demolding your sculpture. The best part is, they cost almost nothing. You can get them on eBay, Amazon, or at a yard sale for under $30. It's a very good investment and a great alternative to buying a foam armature that could break on you.

> **NOTE:** You can buy a full torso mannequin to fulfill your needs. Simply bisect the mannequin by cutting it through the center of the chest. You only need the shoulders, neck, and head.

Latex Mask Making

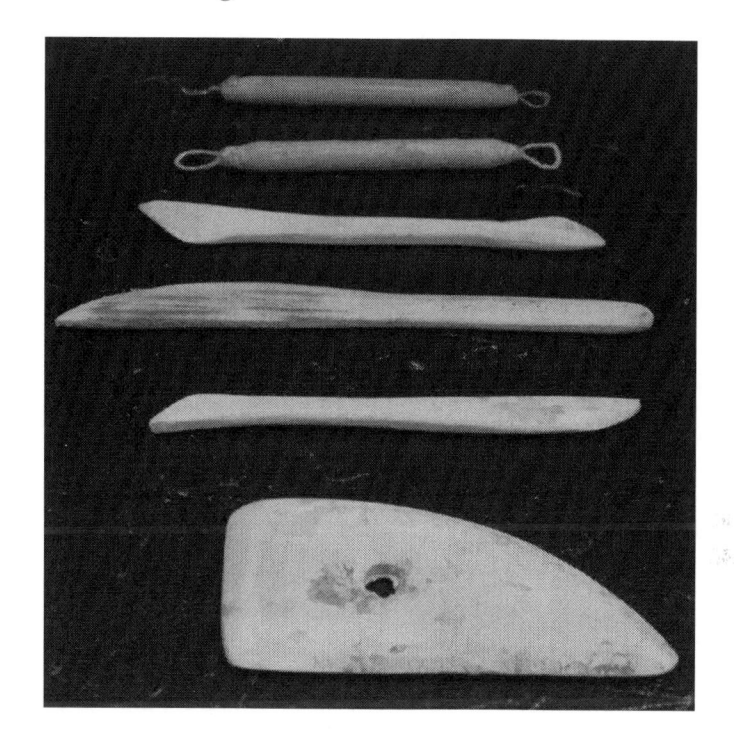

Step 2: Making Your Sculpting Tools

You don't have to listen to me on this one, and I'm betting most of you probably won't. But here's my rant anyway: *please* don't buy your sculpting tools. Try making them instead. The clay doesn't care what's pushing or poking it, so why pay extra for fancy materials and fancier brand names when you can make your own tools dirt-cheap out of practically anything? (Especially when that money would be much better spent on more clay, plaster, and other supplies.)

Plus—and this can be very important for some projects—if you make your own tools then you can create special ones

Russ Adams

that will carve or impress unique textures into the clay, resulting in sculpts that are distinctively your own.

Most professional sculptors make their own tools. I enjoy doing it, not necessarily because of the price, but because of the craftsmanship. Call it a bonding moment between me and the artisans of the past. There is something about a handmade tool that makes me appreciate the work more. I am using scraps that would otherwise end up in a landfill. So by making my tools, I am satisfying a connection to the past and doing my best to stay as green as possible.

The patterns for the tools I most commonly use can be found at the following link www.russadams.me/toolpatterns. If you want to make them for yourself, here's how:

Begin by printing the patterns out on your printer. They should fit onto one page. You may need to adjust the size, but it's not likely. Cut the paper patterns out. Try to stay as close to the traced lines as possible.

Wooden Tools

Materials

1. 1/4 thick piece of wood
2. Pattern
3. Sandpaper
4. Marker

Tools

1. Dremel
2. Dremel Sanding Drum
3. Scroll Saw

Once you cut out the patterns, trace them onto any reasonably flat piece of wood about a quarter of an inch thick. Then cut the raw shapes out. I use Cracker Barrel Cheddar boxes to make my wooden tools. My mother-in-law unloaded a ton of them on me a couple years back, and I have been slowly breaking them down as tool stock. I even use them when I make tools for the students that take my Latex Mask Making and Latex Puppet Making workshops.

Diagram 8

Once you have cut out your tools, put on goggles and a dust mask and use a sander to smooth and refine the shapes indicated by the dashed lines in the drawings. Some of you may want to draw guidelines on the wood itself before starting, to help you control how much material you remove, and where you take it from. A good Dremel tool with a sanding head or stone attachment works very well for this.

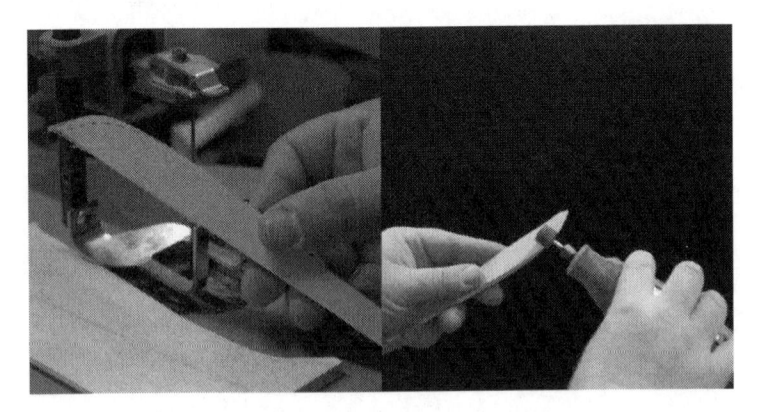

Diagram 9

Latex Mask Making

Of course, you don't have to make your sculpting tools out of wood if you don't want to. You can use metal, plastic, or even fiberglass. You simply need solid material in your hand. It should be firm enough to move the clay without bending or flexing. But remember that you may need to change how you cut and shape it depending on the specific material.

Diagram 10

Rake Tool

Materials

1. Armature Wire
2. Masking tape
3. Plumbers Epoxy
4. 1/2 Dowel
5. Superglue
6. Five Minute Epoxy

Tools

1. Dremel
2. Drill
3. Drill Bit
4. Pliers

A rake isn't as hard to make as you might think. There are a couple ways you can make these. The most common way to use a broken band-saw blade. But I am going to show a method I use. I like to use jeweler's wire and some simple baling wire to create mine. Depending on the size of the loop, I cut a six-inch length of baling wire and nine to twelve inches of jeweler's wire. The gauge doesn't really matter as long as it's pretty stiff stock.

Latex Mask Making

Diagram 11

You want to give yourself a bit of space on either end of the baling wire; about an inch will do. At the inch mark, start coiling the jeweler's wire around the baling wire. Use Diagram 12 to guide you.

Diagram 12

Gently, so as not to break the wire, make a series of bends in the wire to create an Omega symbol. Use the diagram below as an example.

Latex Mask Making

Diagram 13

Cut a three-eighths dowel to a length of five or six inches. At one of the dowel, you will drill a hole using a drill bit that will produce a hole large enough to accommodate both ends of the baling wiring. Make sure the wire is centered in the dowel. I suggest using a vise to stabilize the wooden dowel while you drill. You want to drill at least an inch into the dowel.

Test-fit the baling wire to 1) see that it fits, and 2) determine whether or not you need to trim any excess wire. When you insert the baling wire ends into the dowel, you want it to go in far enough for the jeweler's wire to touch the end of the dowel.

Russ Adams

Diagram 14

When this is accomplished, remove the wire and add a drop of superglue into the hole. Squeeze the ends of the wire together and reinsert them until the jeweler's wire stops at the dowel. Once the glue has had a chance to dry, use some plumbers epoxy to hold the pieces together.

Latex Mask Making

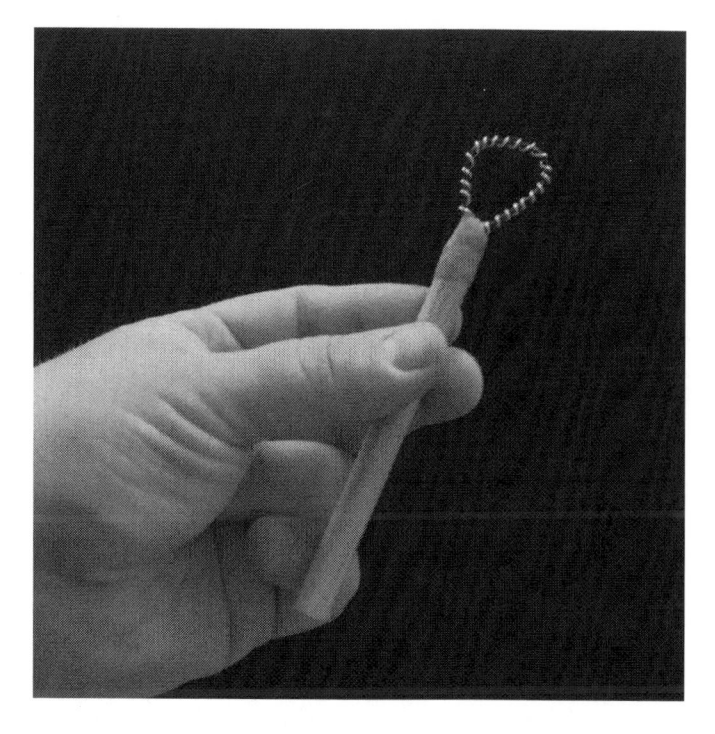

Diagram 15

Loop Tool

Materials

1. Baling or Armature Wire
2. Masking tape
3. Plumbers Epoxy
4. 3/4" Dowel
5. Superglue
6. Five Minute Epoxy

Tools

1. Drill
2. Drill Bit

A loop tool is very simple to make. A three-fourths inch wood dowel cut to five or six inches will serve as the handle. A piece of baling wire or stiff jewelry wire will work for the loop. Drill a hole in the end of the dowel to accommodate the wire. The wire will be bent, so the hole you drill will have to accommodate both ends of the wire.

Add a drop of superglue in the hole, and insert the two ends of the wire and you are set. I personally would add some five-minute epoxy or plumbers epoxy to the area where the wire meets the dowel as an added measure to hold the wire in place.

The wire might come out of the dowel from time to time. It sucks, but it does. Just put the wire back in the dowel with some glue. This is going to happen to you with just about any loop tool you buy as well. In this case, you made a tool rather than purchase one with the same defect.

Latex Mask Making

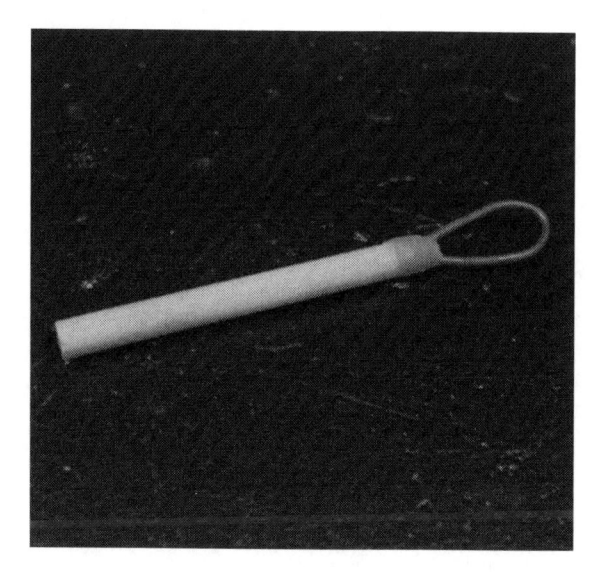

Diagram 16

NOTE: You can also scrape the wood dowel and use the plumber's epoxy to make the handle. This makes a better loop and rake tool. In this case, you cut your wire or blade about ten to twelve inches long and fold it in half (you will still need to grind the teeth on the blade). Use some masking tape to tightly hold about four inches of the wire together. Roll out some plumber's epoxy and cover the end of the wire/blade in it to about the five-inch mark. Let it set. Once the epoxy kicks (or sets) you are ready to go.

Turntable (Lazy Susan)

Materials

1. Turntable Bearing (Home Depot)
2. Two 12"x 12"x1/4" pieces of wood
3. Wood screws

Tools

1. Drill
2. 1/2 or 3/4 inch drill bit
3. Phillips Head Screwdriver
4. Scroll Saw (or similar)
5. Black Marker
6. Straight Edge (Ruler or Yard Stick)

Why a turntable? Like any tool, this one will make your life easier. You are going to need to turn your sculpture around to work on different sides. The weight of the clay can make turning it a pain, and you'll be turning it a lot. In fact, one of the effective methods I have found to regulate symmetry is to quickly turn the sculpture from right to left to observe how things like ears, jaw lines, and temple bones line up with each other. Try doing that without a turntable and you will quickly learn that having one makes life a whole lot easier.

Building one is simple. Again, you want to use scrap wood when possible. No point buying something that might be lying around in the garage. I am going to suggest you build a turn-table that is twelve inches square. It's a good solid size and will accommodate large and small sculptures and armatures.

Latex Mask Making

First thing, cut the two pieces of plywood, or whatever you have lying around. Try to keep the thickness of the wood to a reasonable measurement. Half an inch is good, three-quarters of an inch is good, but one-quarter inch is way too thin and an inch thick is overkill.

Once you have both of your twelve inch pieces of wood cut out, you are going to want to find the center of both. The easiest way to do this is to line up a straight edge with opposite corners. I am using a yardstick. You will see an example of this in the diagram below. Line up the corners and draw a black line connecting them. Repeat this with the opposing corners. You will have a big black "X" on the wood. The center of the wood square is where the lines intersect.

Diagram 17

Next, take your turntable bearing and one of the twelve-inch wood plates and center it over that "X" you drew. You will see in the diagram I provided below there are four corners on my turntable bearing. Mark those with a black marker. I mark them in case the bearing slides or moves when I am working. Next, use the wood screws to mount the bearing in place. The top level of the bearing should move freely.

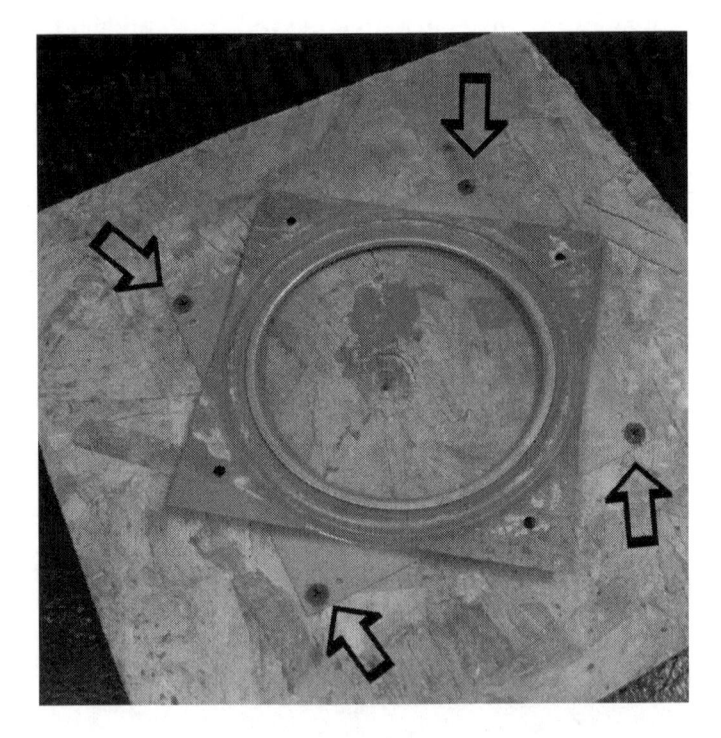

Diagram 18

NOTE: There is a chance your wood screws are longer than the twelve-inch wood piece is thick.

Latex Mask Making

When you screw those into the wood, there may be barbs protruding from the back. You will need to grind them down to prevent them from hurting you, and from damaging your armature or items you place on top of the turntable. Use a Dremel or grinding wheel to work them down. This will heat up the screws. Use a spray bottle of water to take the heat out of it.

You may have to do this with side two of the turntable as well. ALWAYS WEAR EYE PROTECTION AND OTHER SAFETY GEAR.

Now look at Diagram 19. I have turned the bearing so the points of the top plate are centered between the screw holes of the lower plate. It should look like an octagon or eight-pointed star. It doesn't matter which of the top plate corners you choose, but choose one and mark the hole with a marker. Then use your half-inch or three-quarter-inch drill bit to drill out that point. This is the access hole you will use to mount the other twelve-inch piece of wood to the bearing.

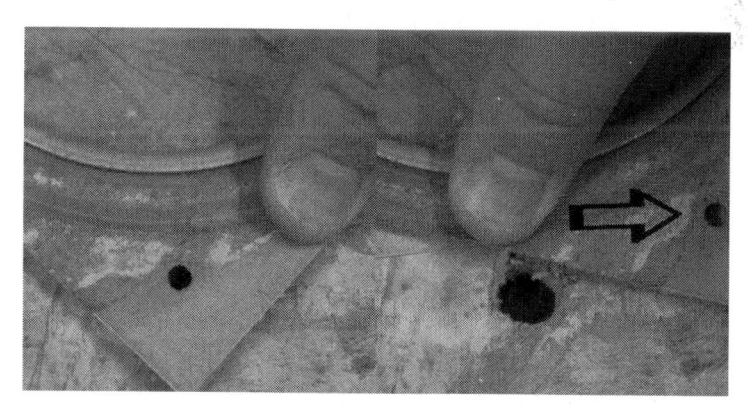

Diagram 19

Russ Adams

Once you have the access hole drilled out, place the second twelve-inch piece of wood on top of the bearing. Try your best to make sure the two pieces of wood line up. Set the turntable down with the UNATTACHED piece of wood down on your work surface. You want the access hole on top as shown in Diagram 20.

Diagram 20

Looking through the access hole, turn the top (or MOUNTED) piece of wood until you see the mounting corner of the opposite bearing plate. This is shown in Diagram 21.

Latex Mask Making

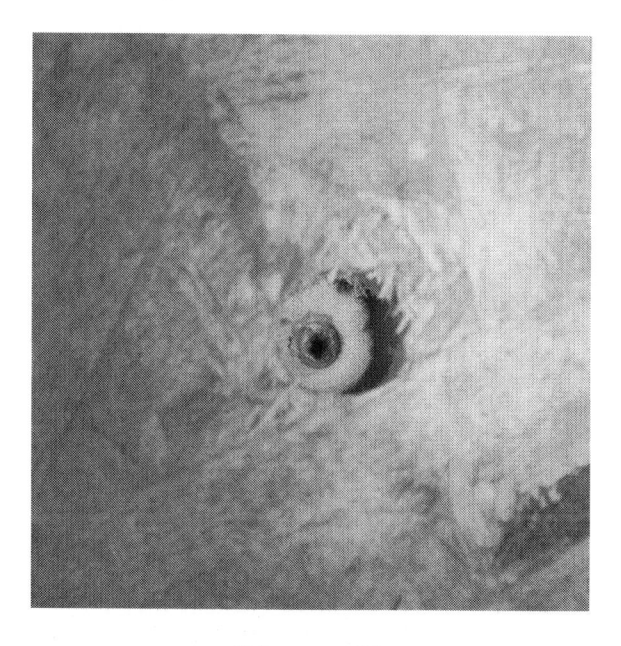

Diagram 21

In Diagram 21 A, I drilled a pilot hole for the first wood screw. You don't need to do this. It was mainly to illustrate where the wood screw will go. Using a Phillips head screwdriver and a wood screw, get that corner of the plate mounted. Then, repeat this until all four corners of the bearing are mounted to the lower piece of wood. See Diagram 22.

Diagram 22

Congrats, you have just added another important piece to your sculpting tools and you probably spent between five to ten dollars. Not including shipping, I have seen turntables for as low as thirty dollars in art catalogs and as high as one-hundred-fifty dollars. This one will last years if you take care of it, and you can use the money you saved to buy more clay and plaster.

Latex Mask Making

Reference Photos

Reference photos are a major contributor to a successful project, whether it's sculpting, painting, or furring a creature. Humans sometimes add or change elements in their mind's eye that are nothing like our subjects. We all know what a skull looks like. We are bombarded with them almost daily. Movies, tattoos, drawings, advertising, cartoons, etc.-- they seem to be everywhere.

If you were asked to draw or sculpt a skull from memory there would be a lot of missing details, added information, or distortions. Certainly, if you showed that drawing or sculpture to people they would see a skull, but it may lean toward a cartoon, have a facial expression, or look like a Picasso. You will do a much better job of drawing or sculpting that skull if you have references in front of you.

It's always important to have something to refer to even if your creature or character is completely fabricated in your imagination. Even an imaginary character has elements based in reality—feathers, hair, teeth, body shapes, etc.

I like to have my bases covered when I am sculpting. I like to have those elements in front of me to refer to so I don't mistakenly veer off track. I look for as many angles as I can in my reference. Profiles, straight-on shots, the top of the head, and the bottom—I grab whatever I can.

I need to be clear: you are not copying these images. You are using them as a guide to ground you in the reality of the character or creature you are making. They are a guide. So you aren't cheating by using these materials; most effects artists do. I would say all, but there is always one person out there that just has to say, "Well, I don't. Never have, never will." There is always one.

Russ Adams

My advice is to do a Google search for "Rock Creatures." Click on Google Images and print the photos that appear closest to the design you most want to incorporate into your latex mask. Make sure you get lots of angles. My favorite references come from unpainted or raw photos, like in process Z-Brush photos. Often the paint and décor can hide details. I want to see those details, so many of my reference images are lacking paint and décor. That said, I also want to see images that do have paint schemes, decor, or hairstyles that I will incorporate into my project after I have molded and cast it.

I will explain this later in STEP 3: Sculpting; but ALWAYS print your references. We are going to be making a horrible mess during this process and you absolutely don't want your electronic devices becoming a casualty.

Once you have an armature, sculpting tools, and your reference materials, you are ready to start sculpting.

Latex Mask Making

STEP 3: SCULPTING

Materials
Sculpting tools
1. WED Clay (Not WET Clay)
2. Paper towels
3. Clear Matte Spray Paint

Russ Adams

Tools

1. Turntable
2. Armature
3. Sculpting Tools
4. Large Trash Bag
5. Chip Brush
6. Modified Chip Brush (Bristles cut by half)
7. Spray Bottle for Water
8. Reference Materials (Printed)

I am going to use numerous photos and written instructions to guide you through this process. I can't determine what style of armature you went with. Are you using a mannequin? Did you buy one? Are you using the plywood and plumbing pipe method? I can't be sure. I can tell you, I am using a professional armature that I made. Mine is cast in rondo (bondo and fiberglass resin mix) and filled with a wood and polyurethane core.

MY ARMATURE: I sculpted my armature in WED clay and used numerous references…much like we are about to do with our sculpture now. I then created a silicone mold and fiberglass mother mold. I did this so that my armatures are all basically the same. When I need a new armature, I simply cast one myself. There was some initial cost up front, but it has saved me hundreds of dollars. I also sell them, so I was able to recapture the cost.

I will also be using tools I made, which are created using the same patterns and tutorials I provided to you.

WED Clay

As I have previously mentioned, we are going to be using WED Clay. WED is a water-base clay hybrid that includes a glycerin additive that slows the drying process. I have also mentioned that this clay is an industry standard, so you are likely to see many professional artists using it. One of the most beautiful things about WED, besides the immensely low price tag, is the clay's durability. WED will dry out if left to do so. It is water-based, hybrid or not. When I am done using it I toss it into a five-gallon bucket with a wet sponge—maybe some extra water depending on how dry it is—and leave it sit for a few weeks and BOOM...I have my clay back.

This same method works if the clay is completely dried out. You can put the clay into a bucket with an inch or two of water. Seal the lid and let it sit for a few weeks. It takes longer to reconstitute it, but it will eventually return to its original state. My advice is to put the clay in a bucket right after you're done using it. Seal it up with a damp cloth or sponge and set it aside for later.

I have eight five-gallon buckets of WED with wet towels or sponges waiting to be used, and they have been sitting there for years. So it's not like once it dries out it's gone, but let's not mistreat it in the first place.

The other thing I love about this clay is its workability. Water knocks down surfaces and smooths it like glass. On the other hand, you can use a heat gun or torch and cook the surface and create some extremely fine details, like crow's feet or willowing wrinkles--those fine features seen in the elderly. If the clay layer is thick enough, eventually it will feed moisture back to the surface and the area that was torched or cooked will return to a softer surface after a short time.

Most people might think a water-based clay would force you to mold quickly after sculpting, but that's not true with WED. You can cover the sculpture with damp paper towels and a plastic bag and leave the sculpture for weeks, although I don't recommend it.

I once left a sculpture on the workbench for two months. I had a string of appearances at comic cons around the country and when I returned I just knew this sculpture was trashed. I took the bag off, and noticed the towels were still a little damp. When I removed those, I was thrilled—astonished—to find my sculpture was 100% ready and waiting for me to continue working. I love this clay.

I don't suggest waiting to mold your sculptures. The longer you wait the greater risk of damage. Forget, for a moment, that the WED clay can, and will, dry out. There are a host of other issues that might come into the picture—things you might never think of. Crazy off-the-wall things that couldn't possibly happen…but do.

I was working on a film a few years back. I needed to sculpt a baby, roughly twelve-months-old. I had never sculpted a baby. The prospect was intimidating, but I did it. I was thrilled with the way the sculpture turned out. I covered the sculpture and left the shop for the evening. The next morning, I knew I had to start molding the little fella, but couldn't face it. So I found one excuse after another to avoid it.

That afternoon, near the end of the day, I was answering emails in my office. Suddenly, I heard a crash downstairs on the shop floor. I ran to the door to see what happened. There

Latex Mask Making

is was. The baby I spent so much time and effort on was on the floor. It was all over the floor, in fact. Baby…went splat.

I thought it was safe. It had been sitting on the workbench for twenty-four hours. So what happened? My shop is in an industrial park. There are railroad spurs all over the place. I had become accustomed to trains going by and never given it much thought…until that afternoon. Turns out the train vibrated the ground to the point that the baby slowly walked its way to the edge of the bench. Then, it took a header onto the floor.

The moral of this story is, you never know when your train is coming. So don't leave your sculpture longer than necessary.

Russ Adams

Build Up & Sizing

The first thing we are going to do is take a few measurements of our heads and, if you are using a human analogy armature, we will be measuring that as well for comparison. Below in Diagram 23 you will see the areas we need to measure.

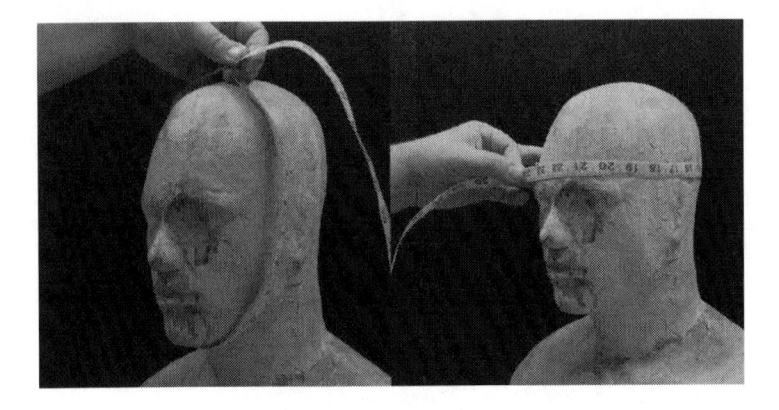

Diagram 23

Grab a piece of paper and a pencil and jot the results of these numbers down. In a few cases, the armature you are using might be larger than your head, but in most cases, it will be smaller. Either situation is fine.

If the armature is larger than your head, hang tight.

If the armature is smaller than your head, you are going to want to build up an even amount of clay across the armature. You want to get the armature about the size of your head so we can build from there. It doesn't have to be perfect, just as close as possible. See Diagram 24.

Latex Mask Making

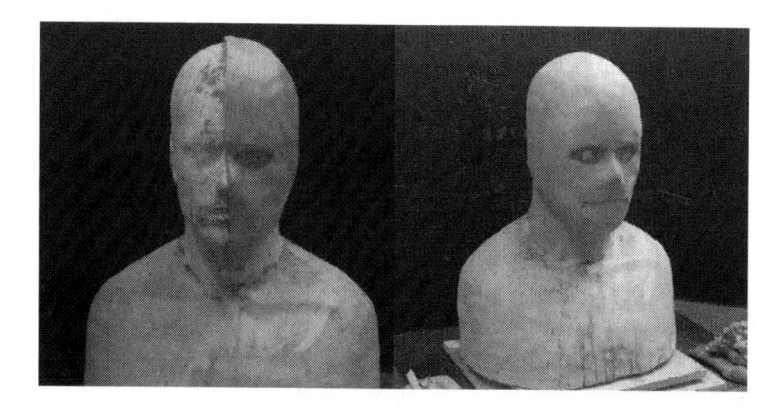

Diagram 24

Now we are basically all on the same page. Our final product is going to be latex and latex tends to shrink. Eventually, we will pour liquid latex into a plaster mold. That mold will leach the water out of the latex and the drying process will begin. This takes some mass from the material and it shrinks a bit as a result. By compensating during the sculpting process, we can avoid creating a mask that fits too tight.

If you are following along with me, in other words creating the same creature I am creating, which I suggest for your first mask, we are going to start building up clay. This is called blocking.

Blocking

What is blocking? It's where you slap on big chunks of clay to "block out" your sculpture in rough, simplified forms. Think of it as doing a quick sketch, but in three dimensions.

In the blocking stage, you build up masses of clay to create structure, then smooth them down with a spatula and rake tool. You will add clay to build up the shape of the brow, the crown of the head, the jaw, the nose, the cheeks, and the back of the head. It's going to look primitive as you work, but don't freak out—by definition blocking is not pretty, so don't get frustrated if your results look crude.

Look at my progress. You will see mine looks similar to yours. See Diagram 25.

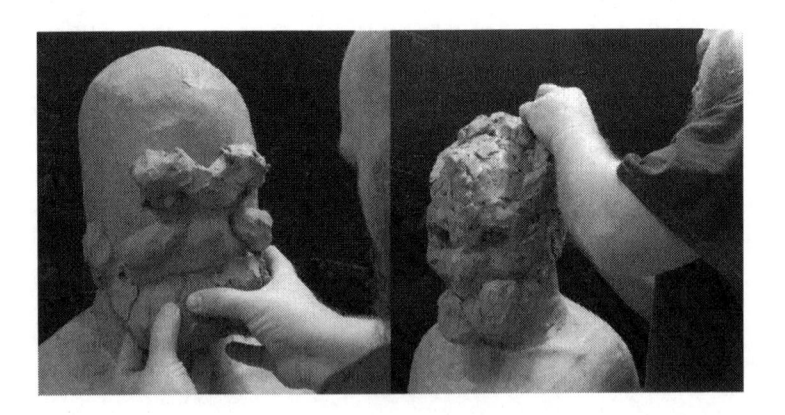

Diagram 25

And don't be in a hurry. Whenever I teach sculpting, I always have to tell my students to slow down and not rush ahead. Skipping a step in the sculpture process often means

Latex Mask Making

having to destroy what you've prematurely created and starting up again. To keep you from repeating your efforts, I want you to slow down.

As you work to complete the rough shape of your sculpture, keep checking in with your reference material. I cannot stress how important it is, especially starting out, to have pictures on hand to look at.

> **PRO TIP:** While sculpting, do *not* try to use your phone, iPad, or computer as a way to look at reference pictures. Print them out instead. Some clays (like WED Clay) dry on your fingers and leave an abrasive material behind which will scratch the crap out of your device screens. And who needs dried clay flakes or dust getting behind buttons of your computer's keyboard? That will certainly muck things up. So, take it easy on your electronics and yourself—*print out your reference images*. Don't waste them either, even if they get trashed during use. You'll probably want to use them again. I keep mine organized in folders for easy access. Let's be green about it…as much as we can be.

Let's take stock of our creature. Does your creature have holes where the eyes should be? It's good to carve out the eyes during the blocking stage so you can keep track of how you will see out of the mask. Does the creature have a basic nose and mouth? You don't need to put a human-like nose on your creature. I will be putting a nose on my sculpture. If you intend to have one, you should establish the structure now. A placeholder is fine.

We don't need a neck, but we are going to make one anyway. The mask we are building in this workshop will end below the chin as shown in Diagram 26. So why rough out a neck? Later, after we've made the mold, the sculpted neck will have a purpose. It will become the tube that will be used to pour in the liquid latex. Having a neck allows us to roll the mold around a bit so all the latex makes contact with the interior surface. When you rotate molds like this, it's difficult to get the latex all the way to the edge of what will be your mask without spilling the material. The neck gives us space to work.

The neck is necessary, but any old blocked-in neck will do. Don't even bother detailing it. In fact, all we really need to do is keep it smooth. This reduces the waste a bit because there is less surface space for the latex to adhere to. Once the latex dries during the "Casting" step, and we pull the latex head from the mold, we'll be removing the neck completely.

Let's talk about the mouth for a minute. Again, your creature doesn't need one, but you are going to lose a lot of character if you leave it out. Think about this for a second. Does being bitten by a creature, animal, or human give you pause? Take it one step further. Does being ripped apart by razor-sharp teeth sit well with you? Likely not. Being consumed and reduced to a mere food product is a terrifying prospect for some. A creature with a mouth full of teeth can up the creepy factor for your mask. Play on people's fears with your masks.

Once I have established my shapes—chin, brow, head, nose, mouth, cheeks, etc.-- I like to refine them a bit by taking either my rake tool or loop tool and knocking down the edges. You can see this in Diagram 26. It doesn't require a lot of pressure. The technique only requires a light scraping of the surface. I will repeat this step all the way around the sculpture.

Latex Mask Making

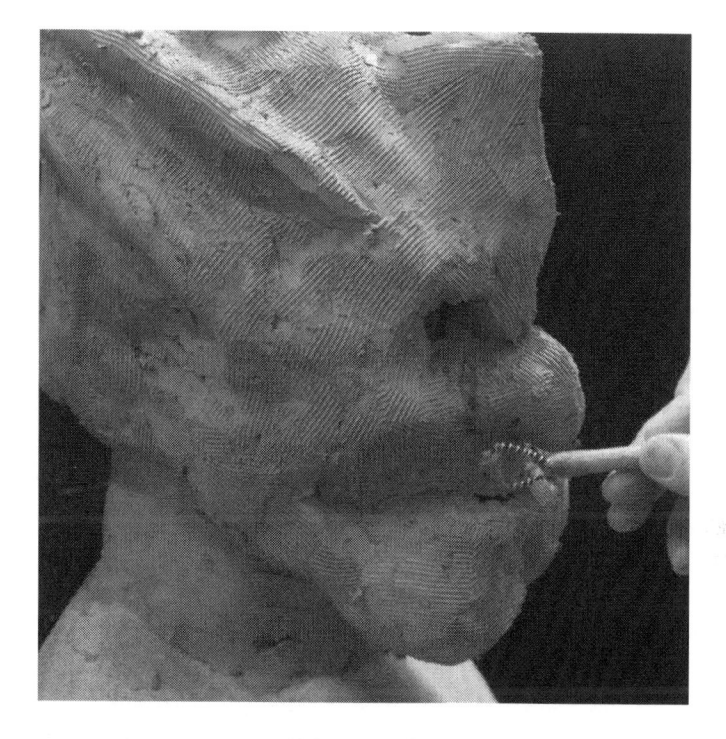

Diagram 26

Once your blocking is complete and you are satisfied with the basic shape of your creation, it's time to move on to the next phase of sculpting: rough detailing.

55

Russ Adams

Rough Detail

During the roughing stage we are going to be adding and subtracting clay from the sculpture. We will be knocking down the rough spots of our sculpture and building up areas that we feel need it. In this case, I will be smoothing out many areas depending on what type of rock I want in that spot. This rock creature is made up of numerous types of rock. I plan to make use of river rock with smooth surfaces, shale with sharp flaky surfaces, crystal with clean corners and smooth lines, and finally stone that appears to have been shaped by tools. Each one of these surfaces will require a different approach in the roughing stage.

I am going to spend a lot of time determining where those rocks will be, then removing the clay and defining the shape with my wood spatula and knife tools. Then I will knock down the edges with my rake and loop tools. I intend to use my larger tools at this stage. I have a small and a micro rake and loop tool, but I won't use them until I have roughed out most of the sculpture. The smaller the tool, the finer the work. Roughing detail is big-tool work.

Each of the types of rock I mentioned comes with different textures, shapes, and ultimately, colors. I want my creature to look as if someone assembled it from a pile of stones, each stone set in place methodically. This will serve a couple of purposes. It will certainly add to my creature's back story, suggesting he was built rather than born from a species of rock people. It will also allow me to demonstrate the many interesting textures and shapes you can use to create your mask.

Knocking Down Clay

Water will knock or break down water-based clays such as WED Clay. If you are using a different type of clay you will need to know how to replicate this effect for that material.

- Alcohol breaks down oil-based clays such as Klean Clay.
- Solvents, such as acetone and paint thinner, break down polymer-based clays like Chavant Clay. Acetone and paint thinner can also be harmful if you aren't careful, so always use eye protection and a good respirator mask when working with these.

Let's start low and work our way up the face of the creature. The chin is a good character piece. Image Bruce Campbell without that chin. He probably wouldn't be nearly as interesting. That chin is over-powering, and makes you question whether you really want to get into a fight with him. Bruce's chin says, "punch me here, and your hand will break." I want that kind of a chin on my rock creature.

I don't want it to be symmetrical, though. Let me tell you why. Symmetrical says healthy, balanced, and stable. When a character has a dramatically asymmetrical appearance, it doesn't suggest any of these characteristics. Instead it conveys sickness, an unnatural presence, and that it's unhinged.

I am going to combined Bruce Campbell's mega-chin with an asymmetrical mass: two huge boulders with one sitting dramatically lower than the other. Now I have my power and that "Oh crap" factor I want. I am not going to add detail to this structure. It's not time for that yet. Rather, I am going to round off the rough shapes.

Russ Adams

We talked about the influence of the mouth and the psychological implications it has. Teeth are a strange feature. They elicit fear, but can easily go the other way. Look at werewolves for a moment. It's the savage dog-like attack that makes them scary. Their teeth are long enough to sink deep into flesh, and they are sharp enough that when a werewolf snaps its jaw closed, those teeth slice through meat like a butcher's knife. But, you can screw that image up pretty easily, too.

I have seen werewolf sculptures that incorporate so many teeth that the creature isn't even close to believable. Some have so many teeth that the creature could never even close its mouth, let alone bite you. I've seen teeth going in so many different directions that a victim of a werewolf attack would be more afraid of being poked by a tooth than having a tooth sink into his flesh. How can you be afraid of something like that? It's a creature that has been neutered on a dental-level.

Instead of teeth, I plan to have a single spear-like knife protruding from my rock monster's mouth. It will be offset adding to the asymmetry I talked about before. That spear is going to appear razor-sharp by the time the sculpture is done. It's going to cut into flesh, but the real fear is what is inside that mouth. I am leaving that to the imagination.

I want there to be an unconscious questioning of what might be going on in this fella's mouth. Does he have teeth? Are they sharp like that spear? Or, are they flat, dull, and hard?

A sharp object isn't always more terrifying than a dull one. Being stabbed by a steak-knife has got to hurt, but how much more pain would come from being stabbed by a butter knife? A sharp knife slides into the skin in an instant. Sometimes, you don't know you're cut until you see it. A dull knife, like a butter knife, on the other hand, doesn't go in so easily. It's

Latex Mask Making

traumatic, it's slow, and it tears its way into the flesh rather than cuts. So consider this in your creature. Mine is a mystery. So I am carving out the opening of the mouth, but I don't plan to show off any teeth that lurk within.

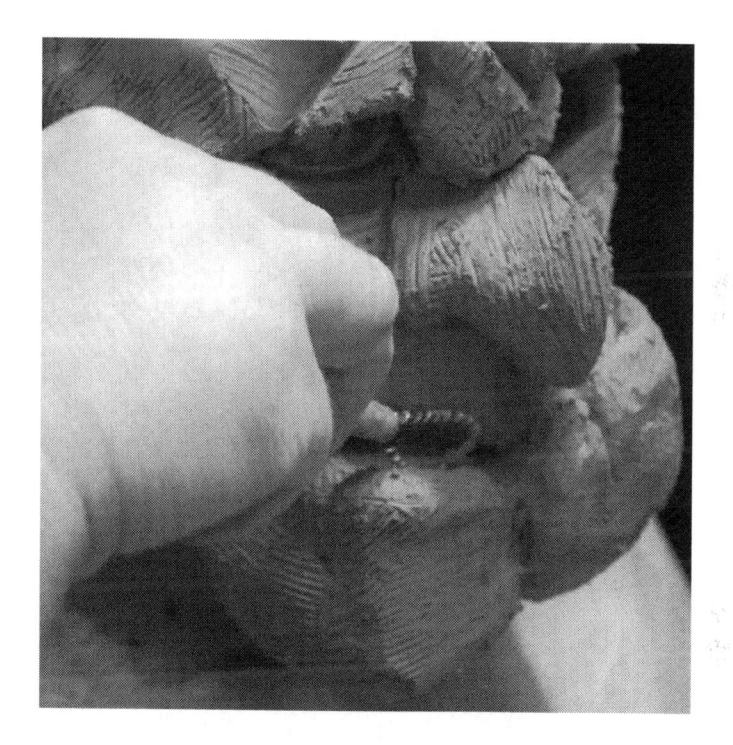

Diagram 27

I like the idea of my creature having some kind of humanoid nose. I like the idea of asymmetry but I want some balance. Unlike those jokers that put too many teeth in their werewolf's mouth, I don't want to overdo it on the symmetry issue.

Russ Adams

I have blocked out the cheeks and raked them down to a more rounded appearance. I also started the crease where the Nasolabial Fold meets the cheek and mouth. The Nasolabial Folds are the two laugh or smile lines that run away from the nose to the corners of the mouth and appear on either side of the nose. In my concept for this mask, I wanted the creature to look like it was made up of a lot of different types of rock. This allows me to get away with some deep recesses between the rocks. So, I want that crease to become a trench that appears to have no end.

Diagram 28

Latex Mask Making

I want the eyes to be deeply set. I know the eyes are the window to the soul, but I also like the sinister feel of deeply-set eyes and a heavy brow. It's stylistic. It's a common trait of my work so it's not something you should feel obligated to replicate.

For my rock creature I am going to keep the eyes relatively simple. I am going to give them a heavy lower lid, and I don't plan to have an upper lid.

I would like to mention one thing about eyelids. Eyelids are so much thicker than people think. In fact, I often tell my students to make their sculpted eyelids almost three times thicker than they envision them to be. A thin eyelid is a sign that the sculptor didn't have a good grasp on anatomy. You might be thinking, "Well, you totally left the upper eyelid off your creature." This is true, but this is a rock being. Who's to say they even have eyes.

The ears are tough. They are a pain to match. Where possible, I will sculpt them on the table next to one another rather than one at a time on the sculpture itself. The first concern most people have is determining the size of the ear. Basically, the top of the ear is in line with the eye- brow, and the bottom of the ear is in line with the bottom of the nose. Look at your sculpture. You should have no problem determining the distance between those points.

Now you have the length of your ear, but what about the width? An ear is more rectangular than it is square. You may want it to be more narrow than it is tall, so the width should be about two-thirds the length.

Once I have the size, I lay them out facing each other...as it were. I make sure to use the same amount of clay to form one ear as I used on the other. I start with a basic "C" shape. Then I use my wooden knife tool to carve and undercut, forming the Helix first. That's the rolled or curved cartilage around the outer ear.

I then start forming the Antihelical Fold, which is the mountain range of cartilage just behind the ear canal. It has a fork at the top and curves downward and connects to the upper ear lobe.

Once I have formed these pieces of the ear, I create two crescent moon shapes…about half the size of the ear itself. This will be the back of the ear where it attaches to the head. I place these on the sculpture first, making sure they match up on both side of the head.

It's important to get above the sculpture so that you can look straight down at the crown of the head. From here you can match the placement of these crescent moons on either side of the head.

By looking at the face and the back of the head, you should be about to match the height of the ears. Once the crescent moons are in place, you can add the ear itself. You'll want to smear some clay around to make sure they stay on the head of your sculpture.

Now that we have roughly defined the major piece of our creature's face, we can move on to the rocky sections that make this guy's head. Look back at Diagram 28. You can see I have started defining my rock structures in a very rough manner. You get the idea, at this point, that this guy is made up of many different shaped rocks—pebbles, larger rock, some oval shapes, and longer narrow structures.

I have defined my brow with these rocky carvings. Notice the deeply defined spacing and the rounded corners and edges. Nothing is symmetrical. The rock structures on one side of the head look nothing like those on the other, yet the

Latex Mask Making

shape of the head is symmetrical. You can see this in Diagram 29, below.

Diagram 29

After I knock down the edges of my rocky structures, I hit the sculpture with a couple sprays of water. I use a modified chip brush to knock down some of my tool marks so that I can see the shapes with less distraction.

Russ Adams

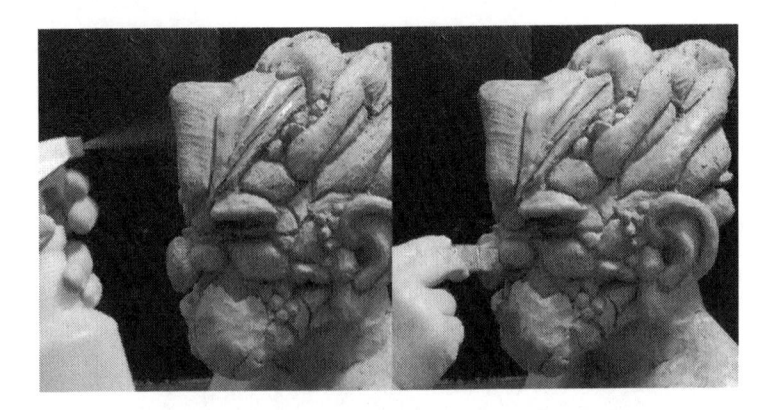

Diagram 30

Don't ignore the back of your sculpture. It should be as interesting as the front. Look at Diagram 31, below. People will be viewing it from all angles. You don't want it to appear flat and lifeless back there, especially in the case of a hairless creature. You never know when you might decide to create a version of your mask without hair. If the detail is there, the option is there. So, take the time to sculpt those details in while you can.

Latex Mask Making

Diagram 31

65

Russ Adams

Fine Detailing

Fine detailing is just what it sounds like: refining the details. You'll want to use your spatula, your smaller loop and rake tools, and perhaps a toothpick to go over your sculpture.

Assuming you are creating a rock creature along with me, there are some anatomy structures we want to avoid. Don't even *think* about adding obvious veins. Veins are a flesh and blood thing. They present just under the skin, such as stress veins that pop when someone is angry. They are the result of high vascular pressure—and one thing rock creatures do *not* have are issues with blood pressure (high, low, or otherwise). There is also no skin for the veins to push against either.

Skin gives a creature a lot of character. Since we don't have skin, we need to express this in the stone. How might a characteristic like wrinkles might play on a rocky surface. In place of wrinkles, we can use fine cracking in the surface of the rock. Think stress fractures.

Think about the inside of a ceramic coffee cup that has been used for years, with all those stains trapped in a tiny network of cracks. These will be most present on the chin, the tip of the nose, the brow, around the mouth, and the cheeks. They might even occur on the helix of the ears.

So cracks of all sorts can replace wrinkles to define age and add character to our sculpture. But what are some other details we can add to rock to bring our creature to life? This is where my creature concept can be helpful. I can use the characteristics of different rocks to influence the look of my creature and bring it to life. Let's work down the face this time.

Latex Mask Making

On the top of the head I have added rock formations that suggest the rock creature has hair, without actually having it. Do you see the way my rocky formations sweep back to suggest a hairline?

Diagram 32

Using the shale-like rock formation I was able to incorporate shadows that look like strands of hair that sweep back on the head. These are actually the layers of tightly packed and paper-thin sheets of rock. I've used the same principle for the eyebrows.

I piled rock onto the bridge of this guy's nose to increase the weight of the brow and give my creature a heavy scowl. I also added a metallic crystal to his forehead. I like to think of this as his third eye.

That heavy rock buildup on the bridge of the nose continues to the nose itself. To me, it looks like a random rock structure on the side of a mountain that barely resembles a humanoid nose-- subtle and bold at the same time. Since the nose seems the most logical place he might be hit during a fight, I added chips and fractures from the impact of a sword or spear.

I used large river-rock shapes in the construction of the cheeks. I add deep and shallow cracks to the rock to add age to my sculpture, much like the hard and abundant wrinkling that builds up under the eyes of older indigenous people.

The Nasolabial Folds and upper lip is where I really added the age effect. I incorporated those smoker's lines into the surface. They traverse that area of the face in a multitude of directions.

I chipped and cracked the Helix of the ears. To me this conveys age, but also combat scaring, and complements the abrasions on the tip of his nose.

Another place I added the scarring was on the spear-like tooth that jets from his massive chin. When you think about it, rock is a subtractive medium. Once that material is removed, it's gone forever…as any stone sculptor will tell you. Whatever battle this guy fought, he would permanently wear the evidence of that brutality on his face. It's not like rock heals, it simply erodes. I will be incorporating that erosion a little more in the painting stage.

Last, I added a little more detail in the chin. Some chips in the spear-like tooth to give it definition and look more like the beat-up teeth, or a monster like the Tyrannosaur. Maybe not everything you might put into your mouth goes quietly.

Latex Mask Making

Diagram 33

Once you are happy with your finer detail, I suggest taking some photos of your sculpture. Take several pictures of the sculpture at different angles. Make sure you get at least one good profile shot of your sculpture that clearly shows the detail of both sides of the head, and a good shot of the sculpture from the top. We might need to review these in case the molding process throws us a curveball. Take all the photos you like, just make sure you have the three I mention.

I am not going to go into photographing your sculpture for your portfolio in this book. This workshop is about making a latex mask, but I will discuss this in future books.

Russ Adams

Latex Mask Making

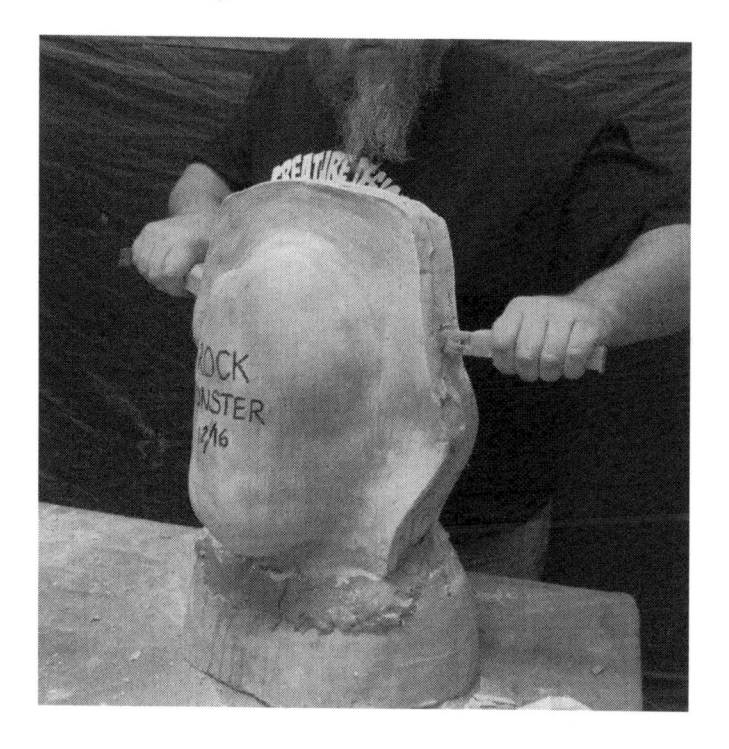

STEP 4: THE MOLD

Congratulations, you have successfully sculpted your Rock Creature!

Now it's time to destroy it.

Materials

1. Ten Pounds of UltraCal 30 Plaster
2. 1 yard of burlap cut into 3"x3" squares
3. Petroleum jelly (release agent)

Tools

1. Chip Brushes
2. A Cup for Water

3. Mixing Sticks
4. Dust mask or respirator
5. Latex gloves
6. Black marker
7. Mixing bowl

I call this the "make or break" step. You are about to create a rigid mold of your sculpture, and there is no way to rescue your work if something goes wrong. None at all. So, prepare yourself. I've been creating masks and props using this method for over twenty years, and each time I confront the molding process a little fear creeps over me. A good thing, too, since it helps keep me focused on steps, timing, and material use.

When a craftsman with two decades of experience says "I have a checklist I adhere to while completing this task," you might want to do the same! I have provided a checklist for you at the end of the book. Please use it to help you remember steps you've read here.

FUN FACT: I use a checklist because I have made so many molds that I get complacent. Complacency breeds mistakes. This won't make any sense to you right now, but it will by the time you have finished the book, and certainly by the time you've made a mold. I was making a mold for a mask a few years ago. By that time, I made a lot of molds. I was working through the process, or so I thought. I didn't discover the grave mistake I had made until I poured the latex into the mold. Suddenly there is latex everywhere.

Latex Mask Making

When I flipped the mold to start side two, I was supposed to remove the clay for the registration marks and leave the clay, representing the pry marks. We will talk about all of these this later. Instead, I left both the registrations and pry mark clay in place. The result was huge holes where plaster should have been. When I started pouring latex in the mold the registration VOIDS were allowing latex to flow out of the vacant space and onto the floor. I couldn't believe the mistake I had made. From that day on, I used a checklist to keep me on the right path.

Timing is critical. You never want to be stuck in a position where time is forcing you to work faster than necessary, so you need to carefully plan your mold. *Never* leave one side of your mold half done. As you are about to learn, there are four layers to each side of a plaster mold. If you have completed two of the four layers, and need to leave your project for the night, DON'T. That's just inviting catastrophe.

Always give yourself enough time to finish all four layers before you leave. Friends and family will understand. If they don't, get new friends and family. Even if you can only do one side of a two-part mold, make sure that one side is 100% completed.

NOTE: Plaster and WED Clay are a lot alike. They both draw moisture from their surroundings. That can sometimes be a problem. A student of mine kept leaving the class to take phone calls. She managed to get the first two layers of plaster onto their mold, but with the constant breaks her mold was left unfinished. Rather than stay late to catch up, she decided to leave the mold for the next day. Everyone removed the plastic bags from their molds to continue working. When she removed hers, she made a horrific discovery. The two plaster layers were rather thin. The clay from the sculpture had pulled water from those thin layers causing it to crack. When it cracked the plaster started to fall apart. She had to start all over again.

Materials are another issue. Always make sure you have all the materials you need for a mold ready and available. You don't want to start the first layer of a mold and then discover that you don't have enough plaster to start the second, third, or fourth layers. Also, don't skimp. Never make a thinner plaster mix because you don't have enough plaster to mix it correctly. Stretching out materials is never good where molds are concerned.

These things are so important that I'm going to repeat them. Call it The Mantra of Molding:

1. Follow a checklist.
2. Give yourself enough time to finish all four layers.
3. Make sure everything you need is ready and on hand from the start.

PRO TIP: First thing, test your plaster. Mix a small batch of UltraCal 30 up in a mixing cup and let it set. If the plaster sets then you are good. If it doesn't set in about sixty to seventy minutes, then there may be something wrong with your material. It's better to find out at this stage than to discover there is

Latex Mask Making

something wrong after you pour the material onto your sculpture.

Russ Adams

Sealing the Sculpture

Most effects artists, me included, use a clear matte spray-paint called Krylon Crystal Clear. I spray two or three coats over the entire sculpture. Follow the directions on the spray can, and allow the spray to completely dry before moving on. Please remember to wear your respirator.

The spray will create a bit of a barrier between the sculpture and the next step. Since the next step can be a bit time-consuming, the spray also protects the WED Clay sculpture from drying out.

Building the Case Line

DEFINITION: A case line is the dividing wall between the halves of a mold. In this case, the dividing line between the two halves of a 2-piece mold (the front and the back).

You are going to center your sculpted head on a clean, flat surface like a table or counter. It might be a good idea to find a scrap piece of plywood to use as a barrier between the table and the mold. This step can get messy.

Please make sure you can walk around the surface on which you are working. You don't need to walk 360 degrees around it, though that would be nice. You should, however, be able to easily access every inch of the area comfortably making sure there is a clear view of the sculpture on all sides. You should be able to work around the whole sculpture without causing damage to it, or the work you put into the case line.

Just as important, make sure it's ok to use that surface. Don't tick off your spouse, parent, or guardian because you thought molding a sculpture on a priceless antique was safe. It would be hilarious for me to hear, but not so good for you. Consider yourself warned.

Take your marker and draw a dividing line on your sculpture like the one illustrated in Diagram 34. Because the line may be difficult to see in a black and white photograph, I have used a bit of intense shading to indicate where the dotted line should be.

This is your guide for the case line. It represents the two halves of the mold you are building. Take care to draw the line on the outside edge of the ear, but don't draw the dotted line *through* the ear. I will explain why in a moment.

Diagram 34

Mark a spot and place small balls of clay on it. Then cover that clay with some plastic wrap or an old plastic shopping bag. Lay your project face up on the platform, with the back of your sculpture's head resting on the plastic bag and the balls of clay. They work like a pillow, preventing your sculpt from being dented. The plastic keeps the clay balls from sticking to your sculpture. Also, use enough clay to ensure the sculpture is level, or as level as you can get it.

Latex Mask Making

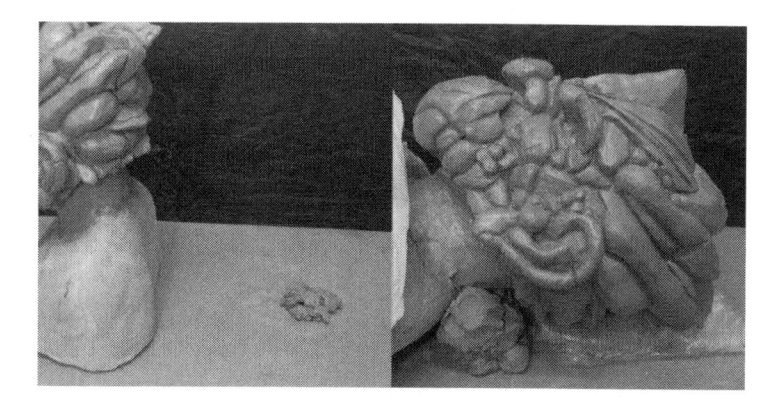

Diagram 35

Now, you need to build a mound of clay up to that line on both sides of the sculpture, but not past it. You can use clay alone, or a combination of wood and clay together if you want to save on clay. Scrap pieces of 2x4 boards are great for this, and cost next to nothing—especially if they were just lying around in the first place.

Diagram 36

Russ Adams

I suggest using a hot glue gun to glue your 2x4s to the surface of that plywood barrier you placed between the sculpture and table. If you don't have a hot glue gun, get one. There are alternatives but they aren't the best. You can use wood glue. It takes much longer to set but will hold in place. Getting it apart later is going to suck. You can also use superglue or caulking, but my suggestion is to spend the five-dollars on a cheap hot glue gun: it's absolutely worth it. You don't want things moving around when you build the first layer of a case line.

Diagram 37

Latex Mask Making

Whatever you do, don't nick or dent your sculpture! Get the wood and clay of the case line close to sculpture, but not too close. We will get closer with the clay in a bit, but not right now.

Did you notice how the dotted line in Diagrams 36 and 37 don't cross the ear? This means that one side of the mold (the front half) will contain the front of the ear, while the other side of the mold (the back half) will contain the back of the ear. To achieve this, we will only build up to the dotted line on the ear, on the neck, and on the top of the head; just as shown in those diagrams mentioned above.

The white area around the ear, seen in Diagram 38, is like a ditch. It will double as a registration later.

> **DEFINITION:** A mold registration is a point or shape that forces a mold to fit together only one way—the right way. Registrations also keep the mold from sliding on the case line. If two halves of a mold slide out of place during the casting process, then liquid latex would spill out, ruining your cast as well as wasting material.

Diagram 38

The area illustrated in Diagram 38 also represents the clay level you will need to create. After the build-up, this surface should be smooth and must be flush with the sculpture. Do your best to insure your clay level is at a strong right angle from the sculpture. This is very important. If you create an unlevel wall, the area where the two mold halves connect will be weak and could break off, damaging your final piece.

Latex Mask Making

Undercuts

Let's go back to Diagram 38 for a bit of important information. Notice how the clay wall contours the ear? You want to ensure that the area around the ear is wider at the top of the ditch and more narrow at the bottom. If this was reversed for some reason, you would be in serious trouble when you tried to separate the two mold halves. We call this an undercut, and it is the kiss of death for a mold.

> **DEFINITION:** An undercut is an area where the plaster surface of one mold half is locked on to the other, which almost always results in a broken mold. Imagine a cue ball. The ball has an equator—the point where the ball is split into two perfect hemispheres. Now imagine that you have pressed the cue ball into wet plaster, right up to its equator. When the plaster cures you should be able to remove the cue ball without damaging the plaster. But if you pushed the cue ball *past* the equator, even a little bit, then the plaster would have the cue ball in its grasp with no easy release. The only way to retrieve the cue ball in that situation would be to break the cement (your mold in real life), break the cue ball (your sculpture in real life), or both. More times than not, an undercut is going to break both.

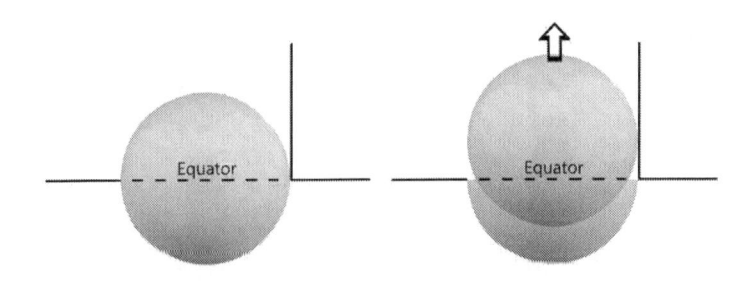

Diagram 39 A

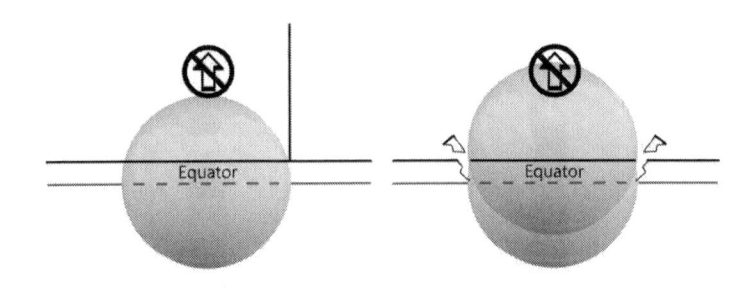

Diagram 39 B

Once we have built the clay level up to the dotted line we can start closing the gap between the case line and the sculpture as seen in Diagram 40. Make sure the clay surface of your case line is as smooth as possible, and meets the side of your sculpture seamlessly. Make sure there are no divots or holes around the sculpture/case line border.

Latex Mask Making

Once you have made this line as smooth as glass, you can move onto the next step.

Diagram 40

Build the Retaining Wall

Now we need to build a clay retaining wall around our sculpture. I show this in Diagram 41. One thing I'll point out is that our walls should be at least 1/4" thick and about an inch to an inch and a half tall. This will withstand the weight of the liquid plaster when it gets added later.

Diagram 41

Your wall doesn't need to be very high. In general practice, the walls I build for molds are about an inch and half wide and about an eighth inch thick. You want it high enough to trap liquid plaster and to make a nice thick plaster case line, but short enough so you don't end up using more plaster than your mold needs.

The next step is to make this wall watertight. We do that by smearing the clay at the base of the wall into the clay of the case line you just built. We are only smearing the outside base of the wall, not the inside. Leave the inside of the wall alone. You can use a popsicle stick or sculpting tool to smear the clay.

Latex Mask Making

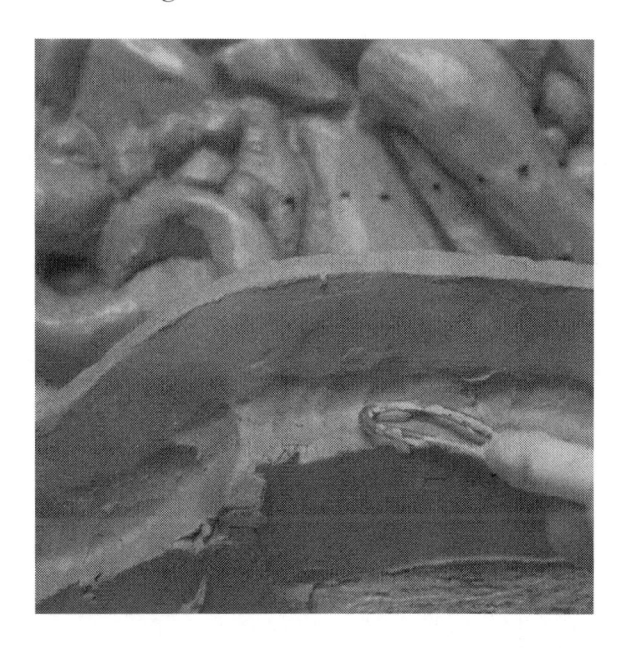

Diagram 42

Russ Adams

Registrations

As I stated earlier, registrations (sometimes referred to as keys) are points on the mold that force the mold to fit together one way—the right way. Once we have the wall constructed, we can create the registrations for side one of our mold.

This is how I make my registrations. I roll out a small slab of WED Clay on a flat surface. The slab should be about a fourth of an inch thick and a few inches square. I am not going to use the whole piece, but I need enough to cut out my shape. My registration is somewhere in the middle.

I am going to use a loop tool to cut out my shape. You might be thinking a knife or a spatula tool would be best—and it might be. I like the loop tool because there is less surface space on the tool itself. The surface on a blade-like tool tends to collect moisture and debris from the WED Clay, which makes the second cut a lot rougher and often warps the line on the registration. Sure, you can clean off the blade between cuts, but why? With the loop tool I don't have to.

Mold making can be a pain in the butt. There are a lot of steps and processes to pay attention to. This is one way to lessen the desire to throw your sculpture through the window.

Using my loop tool, I make a forty-five-degree cut along one side of the slab. I will repeat this cut on the top and bottom edges of the slab. Remove the excess as you cut. Along the back edge, the edge opposite of the long forty-five-degree cut we initially made, I will make a ninety-degree cut. Nice and flat. This is the edge that will rest against the clay wall.

Latex Mask Making

Diagram 43 below will show you the process I just described. The result is a clean and well-made registration that we will place in key points of our case line.

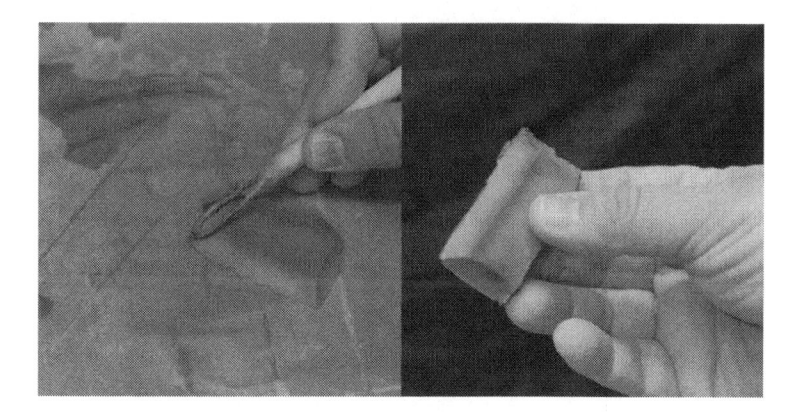

Diagram 43

The next step is to place these registrations on the case line. That canal around each ear works as a larger registration. That being the case, I will use one of these geometric shapes I've just created and place it at the top of the head.

Even if your creature is asymmetrical, where the mold is concerned you want to get into the habit of thinking of your creature as a mirror image. What you do to one side, you should also do to the other. For instance, when you are placing registrations and pry marks, you really want them to mirror each other in terms of placement. If you have a pry mark or registration placed by the forehead of one side, you want to place another in the exact same spot on the other side. Diagram 44 illustrates this point.

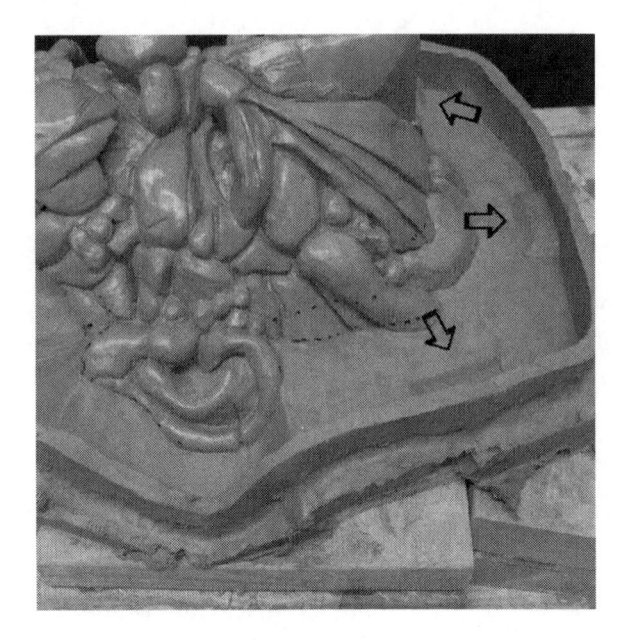

Diagram 44

Once you have placed your registration like I have, you can move on to the next step.

Sealing

I suggest sealing this project with the Krylon Crystal Clear spray. I use the matte finish because it seems to keep the liquid plaster from beading up on the surface of the sculpture as much as gloss does. Gloss spray seems to act like car wax. Ever see water bead up on a freshly waxed car? Same this happens to plaster when you use gloss.

I have seen other artists use gloss spray, then a dulling agent afterward to keep the plaster from beading up on the surface of the sculpture. Why not just buy the matte finish and save a step? Again, it's one of those stress-relieving things I talked about earlier.

If all you have is gloss spray, and you can't afford to pick up a can of matte spray now, you can use it. Eventually, through the process of applying the plaster to the surface you will be able to overcome the beading issue, but it's a pain in the butt. But, if it's all you have, use it.

Two coats of either spray, all around the case line, should be fine. Always wait for the spray to dry between coats, and before moving onto the next step.

Plaster Layer 1: The First Splash Coat

Mix a *small* batch of UltraCal 30 plaster following the instructions on the bag. MAKE SURE YOU ARE WEARING LATEX GLOVES AND SOME SORT OF RESPIRATOR. UltraCal 30 is the most commonly used plaster for making molds that produce latex casts, because of its superior qualities. Never use Plaster of Paris to make your molds. It's a bad material for this application. You will need at least twenty-five pounds of plaster to make this mold. More than likely you won't use it all, but having extra on hand just in case is a good practice. Especially if you make a mistake with a batch and it kicks too fast.

The first and second layers of your mold are commonly referred to as the SPLASH COATS. These are thin layers that capture all the detail of the sculpture. One problem with splash coats is that they can retain air bubbles, which will need to be worked out of the plaster.

Another problem is that these layers are so thin that as they cure they can easily collapse or shatter if left for a long period. As I mentioned earlier, your sculpture is made of WED Clay. WED can leach water from the plaster too quickly and crack it. Once you start a mold you really do have to see it through.

While I highly suggest *you* follow the instructions on the UltraCal 30 container, I actually have a visual process I adhere to which has served me very well over the years. My mixing process is as follows: start by adding about half an inch of water to a large mixing container. I use a two-and-a-half-quart container from Home Depot. They cost about ninety-nine cents and are good for multiple molds before they finally give up the ghost. So as you follow along,

Latex Mask Making

understand that I will be using this container to reference what I am doing.

Diagram 45

Next, scoop out some plaster, making absolutely sure you don't introduce any water into the main source of your plaster. I find it best to sift the plaster out of my scoop and into the water of the mixing container. This allows the plaster to absorb the water in little amounts and reduces clumps. If you want, you can use a mixing stick, electric mixer, or drill to blend the material. I typically use my gloved hand.

Diagram 46

As you mix, make sure to break up any clumps of plaster that form. You want the final mix to have the look and smooth consistency of a thick milkshake. I hope I don't need to say this, but don't drink it. I wouldn't even bother if I hadn't had someone do it once before. Seriously.

Once the plaster is mixed you are at the moment of truth, because after you pour it onto the sculpture there is no turning back.

I start by holding the mixing container over the sculpture and reaching in for a handful of plaster, which I lightly drizzle onto the sculpture. Once the sculpture is thinly coated, I use a chip brush to pull the plaster around the surface, pressing it gently into all the wrinkles, folds, cracks, and crevices. If you don't do this you will have air bubbles in the mold, which will lead to a poorly finished product.

Latex Mask Making

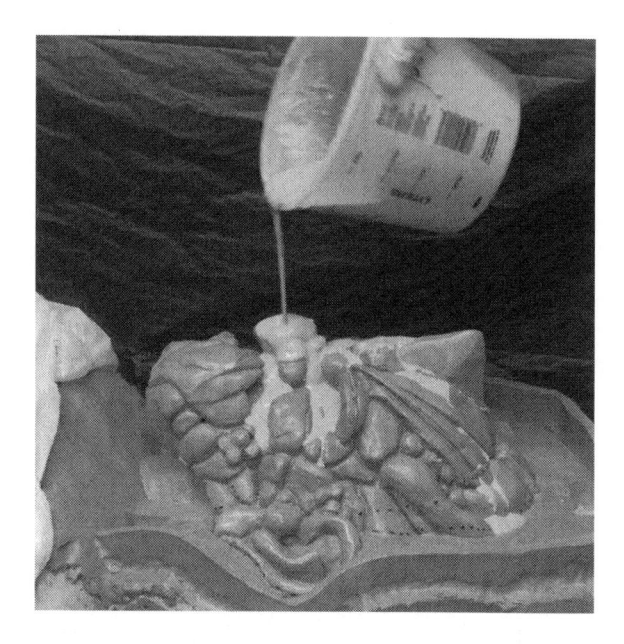

Diagram 47

Pay close attention to the border where the case line and sculpture meet —you don't want air bubbles there either. These corner spaces are notorious for collecting bubbles.

Russ Adams

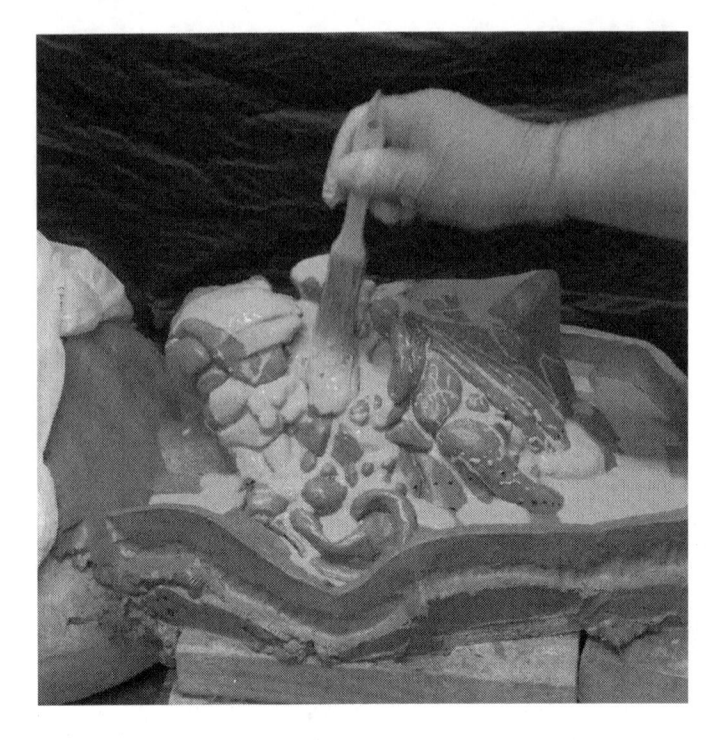

Diagram 48

Keep this up until you have exhausted what you mixed in the container. There's an important rule of thumb here: *if you mix it, use it.* Hardened plaster in a mixing bucket is a pain to pull out, and a complete waste of materials that could have been used in the mold. This is why you should never mix larger batches than you actually need.

Once the entire sculpture has been coated, let the material set for twenty to sixty minutes, and then repeat. Try to leave this layer alone to cure. If you work it too long with the chip brush you will start to remove plaster from the surface of the sculpture. You don't want to do that.

Latex Mask Making

I suggest leaving the layer for about twenty to sixty minutes. This is an estimate which comes with some environmental factors. Humidity and temperature have a huge impact on cure time. A seventy to eighty-degree dry room yields the best results. Of course, plaster will still cure in cooler temperatures and even under water. The more humid and cooler the environment, the longer it will take to do so.

> **PRO TIP:** I call this a "Pro Tip" but really it should be a "Ebenezer Scrooge Tip." As a business owner I am always looking for ways to save money. The cost of consumables, materials that you only get one or two uses out from, can really add up across the board. Early on, when I was struggling just to keep the studio doors open, I would do things like extend the use of my chip brushes. Basically, this meant taking the time to wash them out between uses. You have four layers to each side of a plaster mold. We were using a different brush per-layer. Multiply that by the number of sides, three-four side molds in some cases, and the cost of these brush started to become noticeable. Do the math. That's twelve to sixteen brushes per mold. At seventy-five cents a brush, we were adding nearly twelve dollars to the cost of each mold for brushes alone. We make a lot of molds, so that calculated to a metric-butt-ton of money and waste material. Don't even get me started on some of the other stuff.

So, if you could spend seventy-five cents instead of twelve dollars, wouldn't you? Wash out your brushes. Have a cup of water on hand to get them good and cleaned out between layers. AND DON'T LEAVE THE BRUSH IN THE CUP OF WATER! I just told you plaster cures underwater. If you leave that brush in the cup the plaster sediment will set up around your bristles and you just wasted a brush.

Also, don't rinse your brush or containers in the sink. The plaster will set up in your pipes. Keep all plaster away from all sinks. I always have a five-gallon pail full of water nearby to rinse things off. You should do the same.

Latex Mask Making

Player Layer 2: The Second Splash Coat

Spritz a little water on the surface of the hardened plaster just before applying the next layer. Don't go crazy with it. Just a couple spritzes will work. This is really a repeat of the last step. One thing to keep in mind, though—each layer you apply is going to cure a little faster than the last, because the previous layer is leaching water from the one you are adding, creating—you guessed it— air bubbles. Air bubbles are really a theme in mold making and casting in latex. As I have said, and will keep saying, you want to avoid air bubbles because they weaken a mold.

Wash out your brush.

Once the second splash coast is cured, you should immediately move on the next step.

Plaster Layer 3: The Insurance Layer

I call this the insurance layer because it's how you insure that a cracked mold isn't a lost mold.

Once again, start by spritzing the surface of the previous layer with a little water. I am going to mix this plaster exactly as I did for the last two splash coat layers. I like to lay a thin layer of plaster over the previous layers to reduce the risk of trapped air. I drizzle some plaster on the previous cured layer and coat it with the chip brush.

The difference between this layer and the others is burlap. I have a good pile of pre-cut burlap squares handy. They are about three inches by three inches, a perfect size for this application. Anything smaller starts to unravel and causes a mess. Larger squares tend to bunch up rather than lie flat, which becomes an air bubble trap.

Latex Mask Making

Diagram 49

PRO TIP: Get your burlap at Home Depot's garden section, not a fabric store (unless there is a major sale). Once something is listed for sale as a crafty item, the powers that be hike up the price. We don't need neon-colored burlap either, plain brown potato-sack looking burlap is fine.

Then dunk the burlap squares into the plaster mix *one at a time*. Trying to coat multiple squares just makes a mess. Squeegee off any excess plaster from the square with your fingers, then lay it down nearest to the clay retaining wall. Repeat this square by square, working your way from the case line, then up the sculpture as shown in Diagram 50.

I like to lay the burlap along the entire case line first, then lay the next batch down slightly above it, making sure to overlap each burlap square a tiny bit. I start here because once I have a pile of burlap on the sculpture it is easily to lose track of what is covered by burlap and what isn't. Having a tried and true method keeps me from wondering if I did or didn't cover something.

Diagram 50

Our ever-present risk of air bubbles is worse in this layer, because air can get trapped between new burlap pieces as they are laid down. I use a chip brush to push the burlap into place and squeeze out the air. When you are doing this be careful that you don't press too hard, or you might crack the splash coat layers below.

Latex Mask Making

When the mold is completely covered, the fibers in this layer will hold the mold together if it ever cracks. If it does crack, you will have time to get a few more casts out of a dying mold, or to repair the mold in an effort to preserve it.

Remember: a mold is the only thing you have left of your original sculpture. Once that mold is gone, so is that piece. That makes it important to protect your mold from damage or loss.

Once you reach the top of the mold surface with the burlap, you can rest and wait for it to cure before moving on to the next step. I often use my chip brush to comb the surface down. Those little fibers can be a pill. You can do another burlap layer if you like, but it's not necessary. One will do the job.

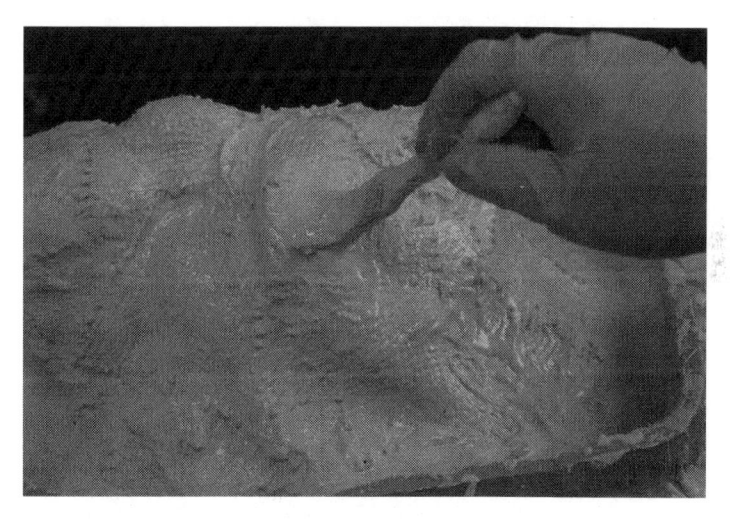

Diagram 51

Russ Adams

Plaster Layer 4: The Protective Layer

The protective layer is the thickest layer. When I mix plaster for this layer I like it to be the consistency of playdough, which means using less water and more plaster.

When I put this thicker plaster on, I am scooping it out of the pail with a gloved hand and spreading it around the surface of the mold. A lot of artists use a kidney-shaped sculpting tool to shape and smooth this layer, but I just use a chip brush. The brush still shapes the plaster into a smooth, clean surface, but the bristles leave a texture behind that allows me to get a better grip on bigger molds.

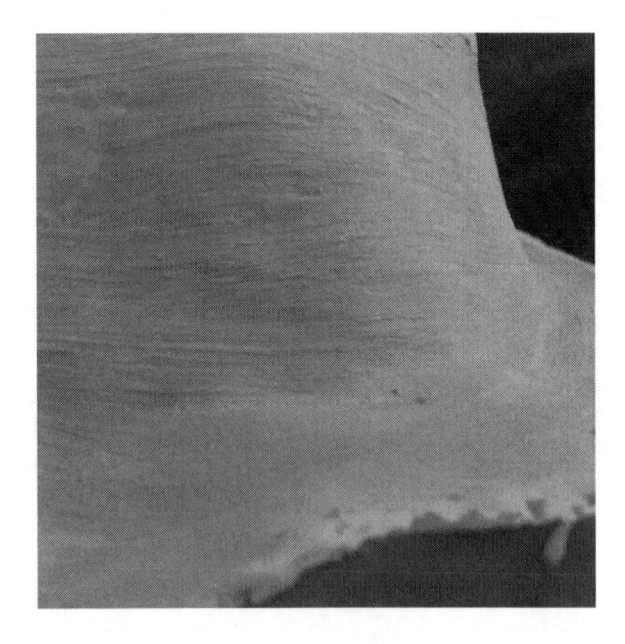

Diagram 52

Latex Mask Making

When you are done, the shell should look a lot like Diagram 53. You should strive to make the surface as clean as possible. When plaster cures, a rough or choppy surface can cause injuries. Plaster edges can be sharp. Also, those rough areas can start to chip and break away, weakening your mold.

Congrats! You have finished the first half of your mold. Let's celebrate! After the mold cures, grab a marker and write the name of the project on the mold along with the date. It's kind of a milestone…a half-way point tradition in my shop.

Diagram 53

Prepping for Side Two

Once the final layer in the first half of your mold has hardened for 20-60 minutes, you can prepare to make the second half of the mold. This is the only time it would be considered okay for you to leave your mold and come back the next day. If you do this, make sure you cover the mold project with a sheet of plastic.

Diagram 54

When you are ready to move on, you can. Begin by slowly removing some of the surrounding clay from the cast line.

Latex Mask Making

If you used a hot-glue gun to glue the 2x4s to the plywood under the sculpture, good news: we can break that bond pretty easily. Just pour rubbing alcohol onto the hot glue seam. That will weaken the glue's hold on the plywood and 2x4s, letting you pop them apart. If you used wood glue or caulking, it's going to be harder. You may need to pry it up.

We are going to turn the entire piece upside down on a flat level surface. It may roll a bit, so we will use the 2x4s to stabilize the mold, as shown in Diagram 55. You can also use clay in combination with the 2x4s to make the mold stable.

Diagram 55

Once the mold is secure we will start removing the excess clay. The goal is to pull the clay away from the plaster without damaging your sculpture. So, be careful! You will need to be particularly careful not to damage your work. If the surface gets nicked it can be easily fixed in most cases. Getting the detail to match up can be tricky if it carried over to the front and it's now encased in plaster. With this character, it might not be an issue and could play to the dynamic. On the other hand, if you wanted it there you would have put it there in the first place. Just go slow, and remove the clay methodically.

We will be removing the registration clay as well. You don't want to repeat my mistake. Do you recall my story about leaving the registration clay in place? This is the reason why I have a checklist on me each time I mold. Get those suckers out of there.

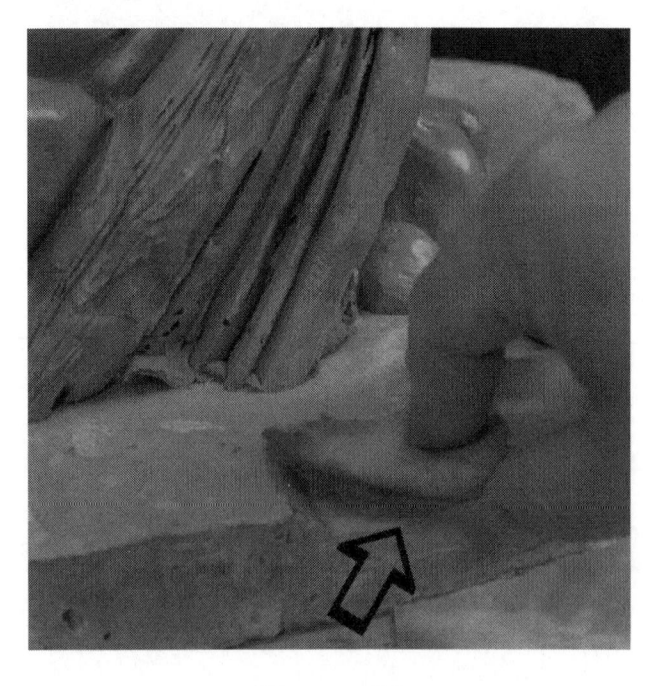

Diagram 56

Latex Mask Making

During the cleanup you might encounter a few small problems. One of these were the nicks we talked about a moment ago. Another problem you are likely to have will be the area around the head where the clay from the case line came in direct contact with the clay of the sculpture. This is going to take some time to clean up. More than likely we are going to be doing some touch-up sculpting. It's ok. It happens, but this is where those photographs you took will be helpful. The photos will be helpful in matching or recreating any detail that might have been obliterated.

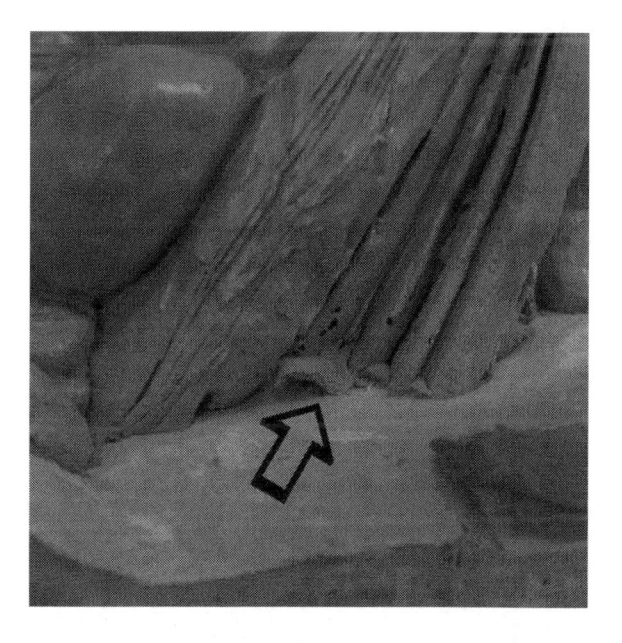

Diagram 56

Once you have removed the buildup, make sure the plaster surface of the case line is clean. This is important but delicate work, so take your time. Use the spray bottle and

109

some paper towels to help. You can also use a chip brush to get this surface spotlessly clean. Any debris left on the case line will keep the two halves of the mold from fitting together perfectly. This can result in leaks, heavy flashing (which we will discuss in later sections of this book), and material waste.

Here is the other problem you might encounter during the cleanup stage. The big issue with cleanup is water. We need the water to break down the clay remnants on the case line, but in doing so it could easily break down the detail of your sculpture. So make sure you are being conservative with the water bottle.

Once you have cleaned the surface of the case line, dry it off and coat it with petroleum jelly. Plaster will lock to plaster, so you need a mold release to allow them to separate with ease. Petroleum jelly is in my opinion the best material for the job.

I apply it with a 1" chip brush for the broad areas, and a smaller paint brush to get all the areas closest to the sculpture—the border where the case line and sculpture meet, around the sculpture's ears, etc. Set the petroleum jelly aside and make sure you are only using it for mold making.

> **PRO TIP:** I may or may not have changed the gender of the persons involved to protect their identity in the anecdote. Each time I teach the Latex Mask Class at my studio, Escape Design FX, I give a safety briefing. Each time I give it, the speech gets a little longer. That's because during each class someone manages to do something that I could never have imagined. That blunder gets added to the speech for the next class. One of the craziest additions has become the most famous. I begin by telling everyone, "This is a working special-effects studio. Nothing

Latex Mask Making

here is what it seems. That said, please don't put anything you find in your mouth."

Why do I say this? We have tub of petroleum jelly in the shop which is clearly marked with a label "shop use." If that wasn't an indicator that this material shouldn't be used for conventional purchases, then the disgusting mashup of debris in the petroleum jelly should have been. A grown woman, *supervising* her teenage daughter who was taking the class, managed to scoop out a fingerful of this filthy mess and rub it all over her lips—her lips were apparently chapped. It wasn't until the tingling and burning that she became alarmed. From that time on, I have asked that no one put anything they might see into their mouths. Label your petroleum jelly container, and don't use it for anything else.

All steps in mold making are important. Each builds on the success of the last. If you don't coat the case line *completely*, even in the registration pocket, the two halves will lock together, which will cost you the sculpture and the mold. So be diligent. But at the same time, you want a *thin* coat. Globs of petroleum jelly will replace areas where there should be plaster. So the thinner the better. Don't coat your sculpture with petroleum jelly, just the plaster. If you thought the plaster beading up on the glossy clear acrylic spray was bad, petroleum jelly on your sculpture takes it to a whole new level.

It's time to reconstruct the clay wall. Refer to Diagram 41 and Diagram 42 to refresh your memory. This time, however, you will want to build the wall a little taller to compensate for sticking it to the side of the plaster. I have provided an example in Diagram 57.

DIAGRAM 57

The first wall was about an inch and a half tall or as tall as a yardstick is wide. This time the wall should be two and a half inches tall and a eighth or quarter of an inch thick. I have provided an example for this as well in Diagram 58.

Diagram 58

Latex Mask Making

Pry Marks

Next you need to create a couple of pry marks. These will eventually be small rectangular channels where a small pry bar will slide in and gently force the mold open. Roll out a piece of clay. If you have a small pry bar handy, the clay should only be slightly wider than the pry bar, and just as thick. This is shown in Diagram 59.

DIAGRAM 59

When the pry bar is forced into this channel, we need the fit to be tight. Too much movement and the pry bar isn't going to be as effective when we force the two mold halves apart. I will explain why in more detail when we get to demolding the sculpture.

Don't place them near the center of the ear, because you'll end up cracking this portion of the mold when you pry it apart. You also want to make sure that one side of the square is flush with the inner side of the wall, just like you did with the registrations. These will actually become empty space in the mold later, so you don't want it too close to the sculpture. Make that mistake and during the pouring step, liquid latex will leak out and make a huge mess. Just like it did to me in that checklist story from earlier.

I like to put two parallel lines on the inside of the clay wall just above the pry marks. A line on either side of the pry marks and an "X" in the center. These lines indicate where the pry marks are. I do this because the clay can sometimes blend in with the damp plaster. This makes it difficult to find the pry marks when you demold the sculpture.

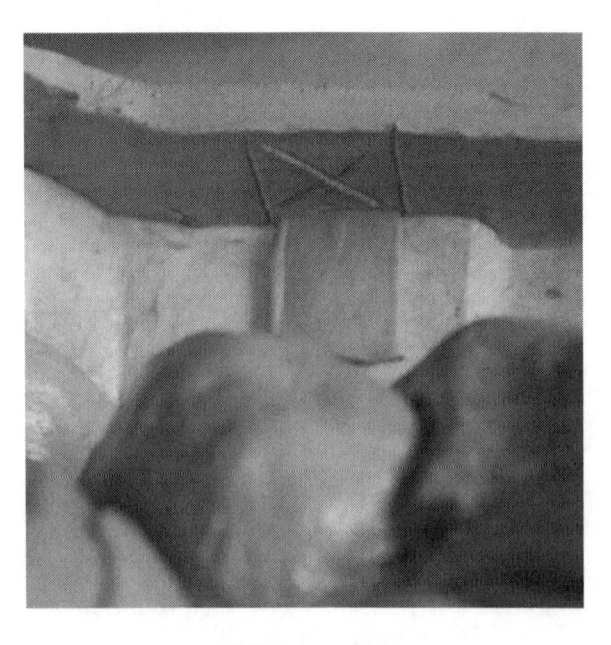

Diagram 60

NOTE: Make sure the pry marks contact your clay wall. If they don't there will be a plaster barrier preventing you from putting your pry tools in to do their job.

Building the Second Half of the Mold

Here we repeat all the same steps we went through making the first half. Once again, wear latex gloves and make sure you are wearing some sort of respirator as you build the four layers all over again.

Rather than rewriting those steps and adding unnecessary length to the book, I am going to ask that you return to the following sections for instructions. Please repeat sections:

- Plaster Layer 1: The First Splash Coat
- Plaster Layer 2: The Second Splash Coat
- Plaster Layer 3: The Insurance Layer
- Plaster Layer 4: The Protective Layer

Once you have repeated those sections, applying the information to side two of the mold, you may advance to Step 5: Demolding.

Latex Mask Making

STEP 5: DEMOLDING

Materials
    1. Water
    2. Paper Towels

Tools
    1. Rasp (or File)
    2. Chip Brush
    3. Wooden mixing sticks (for removing clay)
    4. Work gloves

Russ Adams

Set the mold upright on your work surface. Clear away all the extra materials, such as 2X4s, scrap clay, sculpting tools, and other debris that might be hanging around. All you should have on hand is your mold and the materials listed above.

Remove the clay wall from the side of the mold. This will reveal the plaster case line of the second half of the mold. Now, grab a rasp or file and clean up the edges of the plaster mold. This stuff gets sharp, so be careful and wear work gloves for protection. You just want to round off the corners so you don't get cut up. Use the chip brush to dust off the surface of the plaster mold after you are done filing down the edges. You don't want plaster bits getting into the mold as you pry it apart.

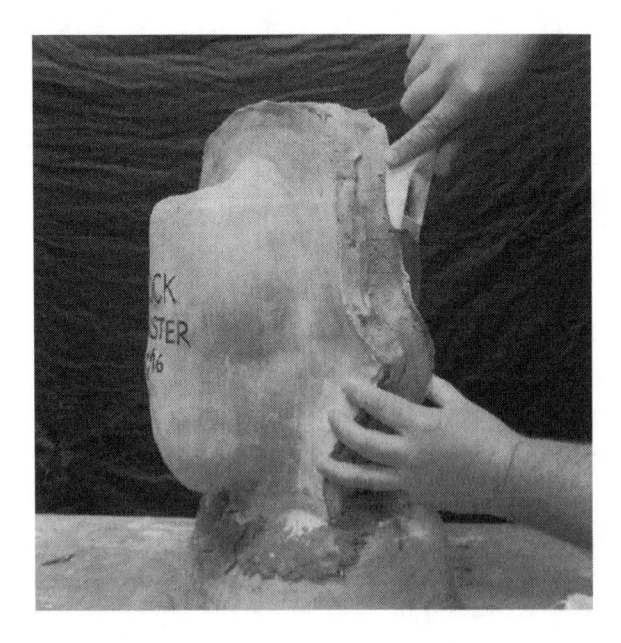

Diagram 61

Latex Mask Making

Remember those lines we scratched on the inside of the clay wall, above the pry marks? Locate those lines on the mold. They won't be indented now, they will look like mound lines on the plaster. Once you find them, insert your pry bars carefully yet forcibly into the clay pry marks, squishing out the clay as the pry bar sinks in.

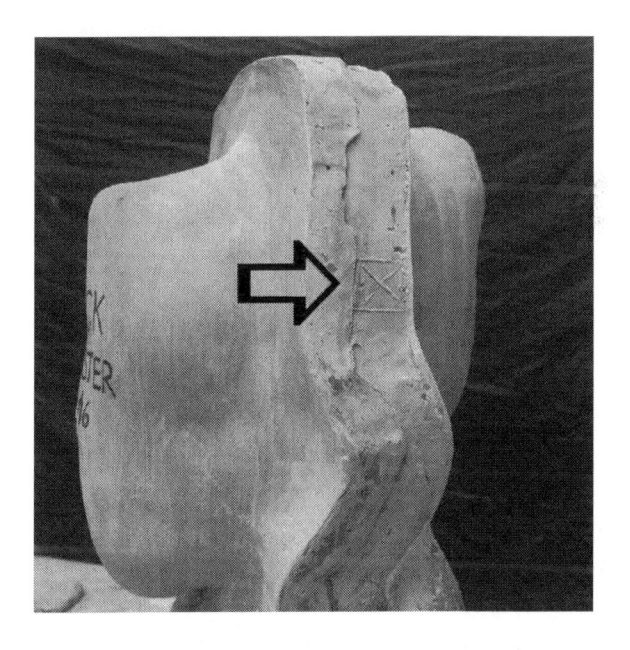

Diagram 62

Remember when I said the thinner the pry slots, the better? The thinner this space is the more the case line will open up simply by inserting a pry bar. If you don't have pry bars you can use two large flathead screwdrivers, but be gentle so you don't crack the plaster.

Now gently pry the two mold halves apart, making sure you apply equal pressure to both sides of the mold so you preserve its integrity. Pry bars are the preferred tool for this, because they are wider and spread out the force while prying against the plaster. A screwdriver has a smaller surface space, which focuses that force in a smaller area, increasing the odds that you will break your mold. I highly suggest you get some pry bars from Harbor Freight or a local dollar store.

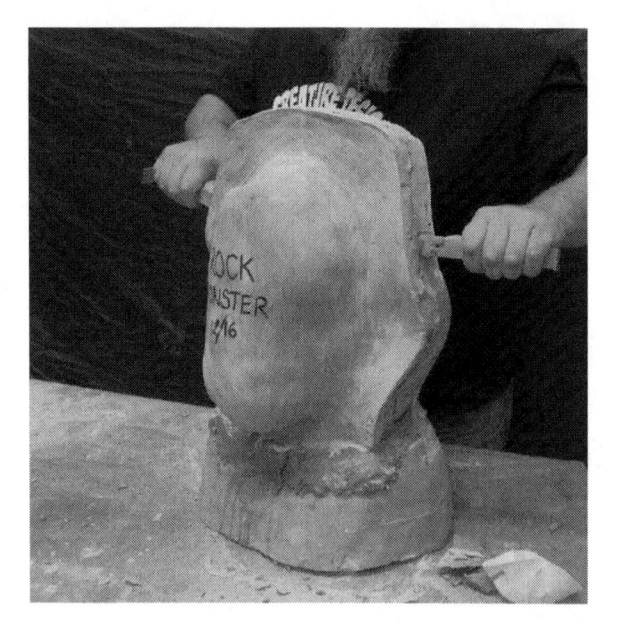

Diagram 63

You will start to see the mold opening once you slide the pry bars in place. If you do, pat yourself on the back. If the mold is opening that is a really good thing.

Latex Mask Making

Diagram 64

Work the bottom pry marks as well as the tops one, making sure if you have a pry bar in the lower right pry mark you also have one in the lower left pry mark. Alternate between the bottom and top pries until you get the mold open enough to pull the mold apart by hand.

It's common for the back of the mold to come completely off the sculpture first. The front will sometime be a pain to remove. You may need to use a wooden mixing stick to clear away some of the clay between the armature and the mold. It may take a while. What you have is vacuum pressure from the wet clay holding the two pieces together. It is pretty common. Don't rush.

Clear away some clay from the areas I suggested and from time to time try to dislodge the armature by pulling on it or

121

the mold. You want to use some force, but not so much you could break the mold or armature. Eventually they will come apart. In a pinch, you could use a little water pressure to erode the clay. I suggest nothing stronger than a garden hose…minus the spray nozzle. DON'T TAKE IT TO A CAR WASH!

> **FUN FACT:** I had a friend with this brilliant idea. Rather than do the work and clean out the mold by hand, he decided to take it to a car wash. We had been working on a film and we were already behind because the director changed the design of the creatures about two weeks before the day. My buddy, a lazy and stupid-stupid-stupid man, headed to a local car wash. His plan was to brace the mold to keep it from moving while he used the high-pressure water to remove the clay. It worked like a charm. Or so he thought. The clay came flying out of the mold. He was ecstatic…until the water was turned off. Turns out the mold had an air bubble that was trapped between the burlap layer and the two splash coats. When the high-pressure water hit the mold, it punched through that thin plaster splash coat, exposing an air hole. It didn't stop there. The pressure must have forced the surrounding splash coat to peel away. More and more of the plaster was ripped out.
>
> When he shut the water off he started to see flecks of gray plaster bits all over the stall like confetti at a parade. Upon inspection of the mold, he discovered there was no more detail in it. The moron had ripped most of it out. Had he cleaned the mold out properly we would have discovered the air pocket and fixed it. Hell, the plaster might have held and we might have gotten several casts before it became a problem. Instead, we got to redo the entire thing.

Latex Mask Making

You might get away with it once, maybe twice. At some point, it's going to catch up with you and screw up a week's worth of work. The moral of the story is don't be a lazy idiot. Clean the mold out the right way.

Once the mold is apart and your armature is tucked away, clean all the clay out of the mold—i.e., your sculpture. Use wooden tools to remove the clay instead of metal ones, because wooden tools are less likely to scratch the surface of your mold. You can use water to help break down the clay.

Diagram 65

123

Russ Adams

DON'T USE YOUR SCULPTING TOOLS FOR A CLEAN-OUT! The process will destroy your newly created wooden tools. Instead, use the wooden mixing sticks to remove the clay mess.

You can save a lot of the clay for reuse if you are careful. Once you have removed the clay, use a toothbrush or a chip brush and warm water to clean out any residue.

This clean-out will take a while, so be patient. If mold making is evil, then the clean-out is its baby brother. It sucks, but it's part of the gig. There might be a moment when you think you have it all cleaned out. I am betting you have more clay inside. If you think you're done, walk away from the project for a day and let the plaster dry. Come back the next morning and spray some water into the mold surface. That darker stuff is clay. Get it out of there.

If everything looks good, pat yourself on the back. Well done! If not, start over again at Step 1 and consider this lost project a learning experience. You didn't fail if you learned something.

Latex Mask Making

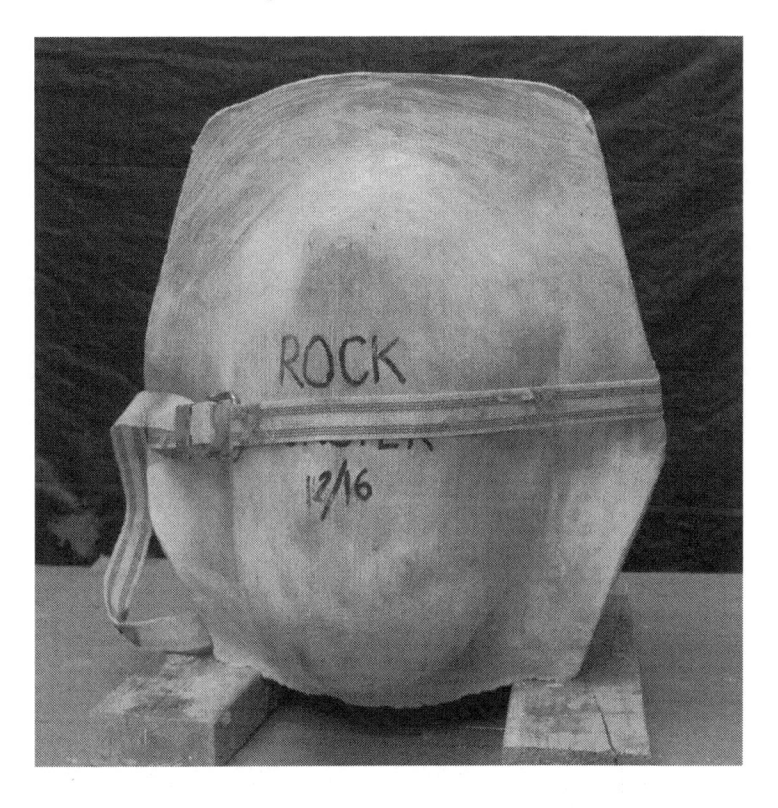

STEP 6: LATEX CASTING

Materials

    1. One gallon of Mask Latex
    2. Clear Ammonia (Optional)

Tools

    1. Mold Straps
    2. 2x4s

Let your mold halves dry for at least a week before trying to cast. The mold may be cured, but it's not dry. The mold works by pulling the water out of the latex. If the mold isn't dry, then it can't pull any water out and you will be left with a horrible mess on your hands. (DON'T ATTEMPT TO SPEED THE MOLD-DRYING PROCESS BY BAKING OR HEATING THE MOLD. All you will do is crack or weaken it.)

> **FUN FACT:** We often use molds like these for foam latex makeup appliances, where you have to gently bake the foam latex in the mold. One day, after a long cool-down process—about 3 hours—I took a mold out of a 90-degree oven into a 75-degree work space. I got all of two feet away from the oven when the mold shattered in my hands. That 15-degree difference in heat turned a week of work to trash within a tenth of a second. You don't need to heat your mold. You just have to be patient!

When it's finally time to cast, put your mold halves together and secure them with mold straps. You can buy them for a few dollars at a ceramics supply store or a hobby store, and you might even find them on Amazon. They are a wise investment at three or four dollars.

I don't have a creative replacement for them. They are the best tool for the job. Don't try using rubber bands or cargo straps. The rubber bands stretch, and if your mold is big enough the weight of the latex can stretch them out enough to leak material everywhere. The latches on a cargo strap tend to put a focused strain on the mold and can crack it.

Latex Mask Making

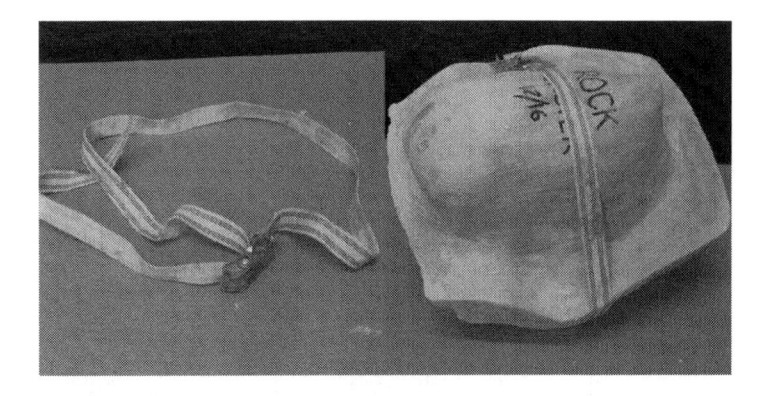

Diagram 66

Once the mold is locked tightly together with the mold straps, set it on a work surface with the neck hole facing up. Slowly pour your latex into the neck of the mold, tapping the sides of the mold with the palm of your hand to disengage any air bubbles that form.

I usually pause when I have filled the mold about half way. At this point I will turn the mold a few times as to coat the entire inner surface of the mold with liquid latex. Then I continue filling the mold to the neck line.

Fill the mold completely. Give it about 15-20 minutes. You can even go to 45 minutes, but that's a really thick mask. Pour the remaining latex back into the pail. Place two pieces of wood under the mold with the neck hole facing down (see Diagram #). Then go away and do something else while the latex solidifies and drains.

I let the mold drain for about twenty to thirty minutes, then close my bucket of latex and set the mold on the bench to dry overnight.

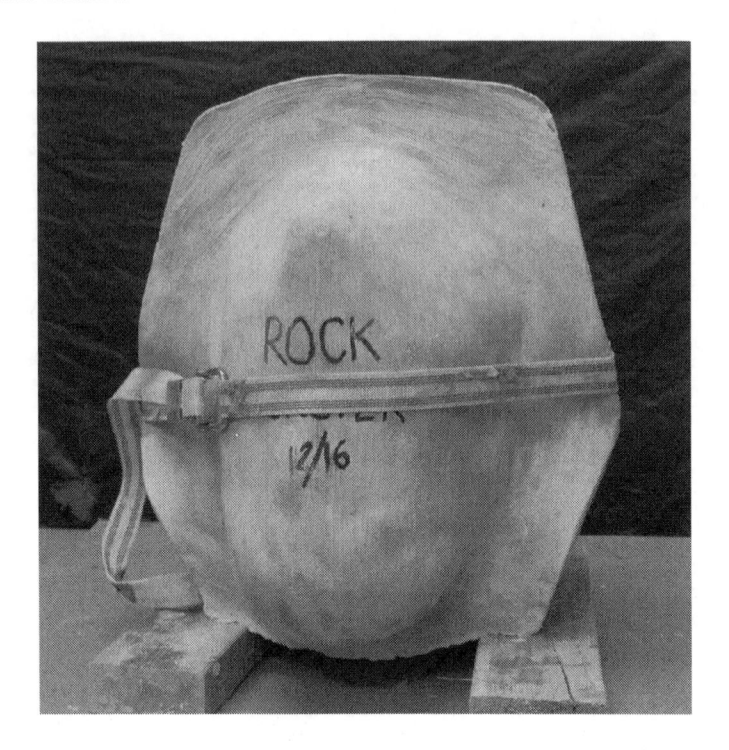

Diagram 67

PRO TIP: When latex has been sitting for a few weeks, or even months, it will start to lose water and thicken up. This thicker latex is a pain to pour into a mold. It doesn't so much flow into the mold as it plops in. The thicker material also allows air bubbles to become trapped. They can't escape through the thicker material and they tend to hang out in places that will ruin your day.

To revitalize your latex, add some clear ammonia to the mix, about a capful to a gallon at first. Mix the ammonia into the latex. If it thins the material out enough to get a more user-friendly pour, then great. If

Latex Mask Making

not, add another capful. You don't want to overdo it, though.

I suggest getting the clear ammonia from the cleaning aisle at the dollar store. If might take you years to use it all, but it's good to have nearby for latex work.

In the summer, you should be able to demold your cast the next morning. If it's spring or fall, you might have to wait another day. In the winter, you're more likely to wait two or three days.

Diagram 68

Russ Adams

When the latex is dry, remove the mold straps, and use your pry bars to gently pry the mold open. Once again, remember to apply equal pressure on both side of the mold. Once the mold halves are apart, you can peel out your latex CAST and get it ready for cleaning and seam work. (Casts are also referred to as "pulls.")

Latex Mask Making

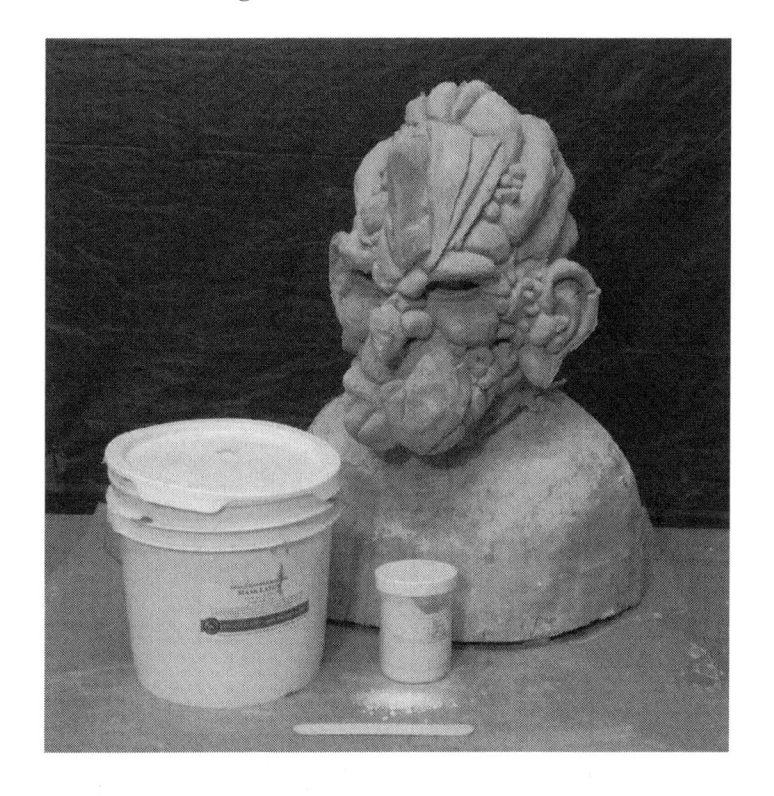

STEP 7: SEAMING & CLEANING

Materials
1. Latex and
2. Cabosil
3. Mixing sticks
4. Mixing cup

Tools
1. Fingernail scissors
2. Dremel Tool
3. Dremel Stone or Buffing Bit

Russ Adams

Completing your mask involves seaming, cleaning, and various kinds of finishing. You might not think so, but these are very important steps. We will patch air bubble issues that might have occurred. We will clean up the seams that are caused by the case lines and remove the debris on the latex before we move onto the finishing work. Skip these steps and your work of art will suffer.

Latex Mask Making

Seaming

Seaming is the art of removing any excess material left behind in the casting process, grinding down the evidence of that material, and filling it in with raw latex and cabosil (also called cabopatch).

The first thing you may notice when you remove your cast from the opened mold is a thin line of extra material around the whole piece as seen in Diagram 69. This is called "flashing."

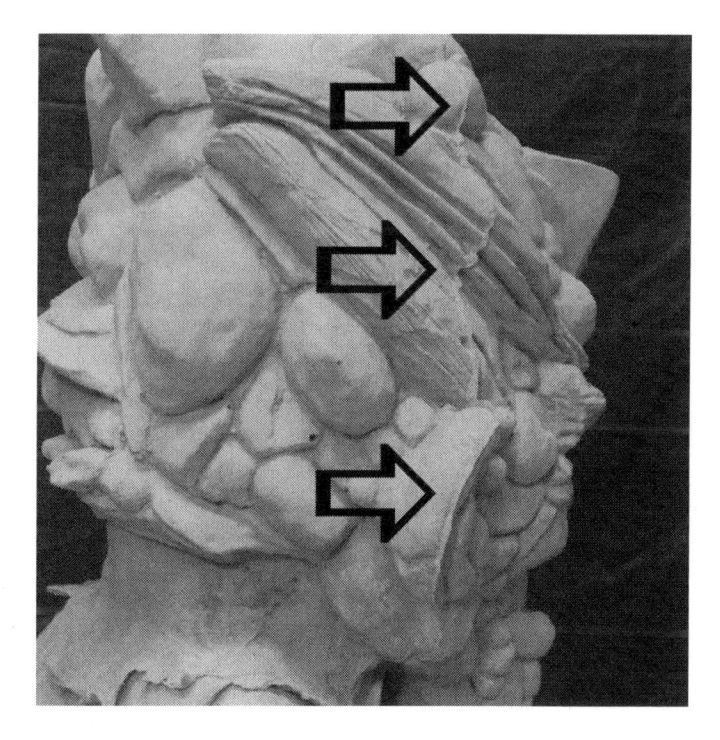

Diagram 69

Basically, flashing is what happens when the straps don't hold the mold together tightly enough, or there was debris on the case line of the mold that prevented it from closing completely. In more serious cases the problem could be related to a poor mold construction. In all of these cases, the flashing is caused by a gap between the case lines, which allowed liquid latex to leak between the two mold halves. It's common for this to happen with a mold, especially a first mold.

On the plus side, if you got a latex pull out of your mold and didn't have a ton of latex leaking onto the floor, then you have a successful project. We just have to tune up your skills a bit, but that comes with practice.

Flashing can be removed with a pair of sharp scissors. I know I keep talking about making your tools, not buying them, but this is where that money you saved can be well invested. I use Tweezerman Fingernail Scissors to remove the flashing. These are great scissors and I only use them on latex—nothing else. Tweezerman Scissors will set you back twenty-five to thirty-five dollars, but they do a great job and last a long time. I have had mine roughly four years or more. I bought mine after using them on Jim Henson's Creature Shop Challenge. You can buy less expensive fingernail scissors to do the job. In my experience, I was replacing them within a few weeks. In defense of the cheaper scissors, I do use them a lot.

The reason I use fingernail scissors is because of the curve. I use that curve to follow the contour of the mask's surface. You don't want to get too close to the mask when you are removing the flashing. Too close and you could cut deep enough to create a hole in the mask. So leave about 1/16 of an inch behind and we will grind off the rest.

Latex Mask Making

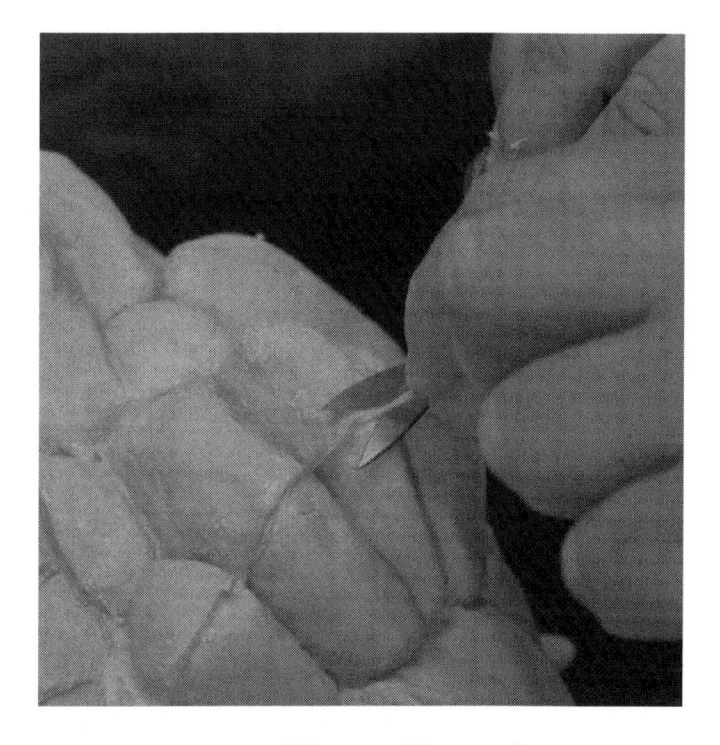

Diagram 70

Once you remove the flashing, the seam can be ground away using a Dremel tool and either a stone bit or a buffing bit. If I use a stone bit, I use a round stone bit. I mostly use a buffing bit for this, but it's a personal preference, not quality related. I set the Dremel on a medium speed and gently grind away the seam using a small circular pattern. It's important to take your time and be vigilant. There are two major problems that could occur when you are grinding off the seam:

1. You could grind the seam down too far with your Dremel. This might wear a hole in the surface of the mask. This might even occur because you hit an unforeseen air bubble

trapped in the latex. If this does happen, don't panic. You can fill the hole with Cabopatch. Let the patch dry and use the Dremel to smooth the surface. Always let the Cabopatch dry completely before grinding off the rough area.

2.Sometimes your mask can get wrapped around the Dremel. It happens when you set the Dremel speed too high and the latex catches the bit and before you can react the mask is coiled around the Dremel bit. This is perhaps the most damaging issue to deal with when using a Dremel to remove seams from a mask. If this happens it can, and often does, cause irreparable damage to the mask. When the mask wraps up like this it stretches and twists the latex so badly that the latex often times won't rebound. So, to decrease the chances of having this happen to you, set the Dremel to a medium speed. Yes, it takes longer to finish the seaming, but at least you aren't sacrificing the mask to the rotary-tool gods.

Latex Mask Making

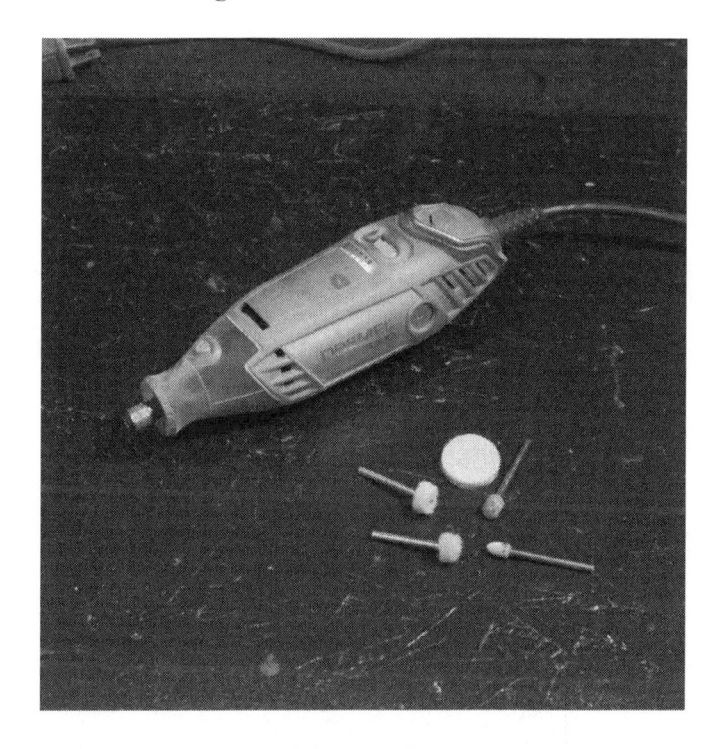

Diagram 71

Cleaning

Cleaning is next. When you remove a pull (or cast) from a mold, especially a plaster mold, the cast often has plaster dust on the latex. It's actually part of your mold that has been pulled away by the latex. This is common and the reason why plaster molds have a limit to the number of pulls they can produce. With each pull, the mold loses a little more detail and material. So just be prepared.

This plaster debris needs to be scrubbed off the cast so you can paint the mask. The other material that might very well be present is clay. It might be as simple as clay dust or it might be that you missed some clay during the mold clean-out. If you do have a chunk of clay in your mask, go ahead and remove it. It may have left a hole or cavity in your mask. Go ahead and use the Cabopatch to fix it. You will have to wait for the Cabopatch to dry completely before you clean the mask, but that's part of the charm of latex mask making.

I use dish soap and a chip brush to clean the surface of a mask. I cut down the bristles of the chip brush by about half. This makes the brush stiffer and helps to get the surface good and clean. I scrub the cast thoroughly, then put it on a human analog armature to dry.

I dry the mask on an armature to prevent it from warping. If you simply hang the mask to dry, gravity will pull it into a shape that you didn't intend and you may find it difficult to correct. If you don't have a human analog armature or mannequin to dry it on, try stuffing it with newspaper so that it can hold its intended shape.

Latex Mask Making

NOTE: You don't need to soak the mask. You only want to dampen the surface. If you get it too wet, it will make drying the mask difficult. It will still dry out, but it might warp the shape or take days.

Russ Adams

Latex Mask Making

STEP 8: FINISHING WORK

Materials
    1. Acrylic paints
    2. Clear Matte or Gloss Acrylic Spray Paint
    3. Water

Tools
    1. Assorted Paint Brushes
    2. Sponges

Russ Adams

When making latex masks there are two fun stages and one pain in the butt. Sculpting is a blast—it's a process you can get lost in and enjoy. Molding is the pain. You have to do it. It's a necessary evil, but oh my gods it's messy and back-breaking. But molding is a critical part of the process and an art form unto itself. It's so important that I don't trust anyone to mold one of my sculptures. Finishing, on the other hand, is arguably the most fun of all. It's the whole process of painting, furring, and adorning your creature, or transforming it from a raw latex pull into a finished thing of beauty (or beautiful creepiness).

Concept

Before you start painting your mask, seriously study your photo references and think about this project, the Rock Creature. Look at tons of rock references. Hell, there is probably some good example in your yard. Check out the coloring of the rocks. What's on them? Does your concept have lichens on it? Lichens are those fungal, algal crusts colonizing the surface of rocks, boulders, and possibly your sidewalk and driveway. These things are amazing accents that will make your mask pop.

Does your rock creature have moss on it? These and other colorful additions bring a flat creature kicking and screaming into the real world. It gives him a visual backstory. The same can be said for any mask you create. Look past the overall and into the details. This is just as important as the base paint job.

Washes

With that lovely thought in mind, we need to start painting the base. We do this with few washes. In case you don't know, washes are thin mixtures of paint… generally equal parts water and paint. Sometimes they can be more water than paint. It depends on what you are looking for. In this case, we just want to stain the surface and make the cracks and detail pop.

Again, we are staining the latex one layer at a time. Make sure you are wearing latex gloves, because this is going to be messy. Real messy!

I am going to use two colors for a wash that will stain the latex. I am using black and blue-greys. Black is your best bet as a base because it gets trapped in the cracks and channel we sculpted. You don't have to go black, though. You can achieve a really good look using those blues and greys. It's a rock creature so I am going for cooler tones.

I generally mix 2-parts water to 1-part acrylic paint to create my washes. I use a chip brush to apply them, ensuring the entire pull is covered. Using the chip brush, I work the paint into the cracks. You can't always count on the paint to just flow into those areas. Never discount the power of an air bubble, even in the paint process. The brush can help push the air bubble around and out of the way of the paint. I apply several coats of these washes, blotting away paint each time. In the case of my rock creature, I am going to allow some paint to run.

Russ Adams

When I have the mask covered, I use a damp sponge or cloth to dab off the paint I just added to the mask. This lets me control the amount of paint I have on the mask, but also starts the mottling process. Mottling is a blotchy break-up of colors. The best example I can give you is to look at your forearm or the palm of your hand. Do you see how blotchy the colors are? It's natural…of course it's natural. It's on your hand. Newcomers often discount mottling in their paint job when they are making creature masks. They are fixated on the predominate solid colors they see. Their creatures end up looking more like a cartoon because of it.

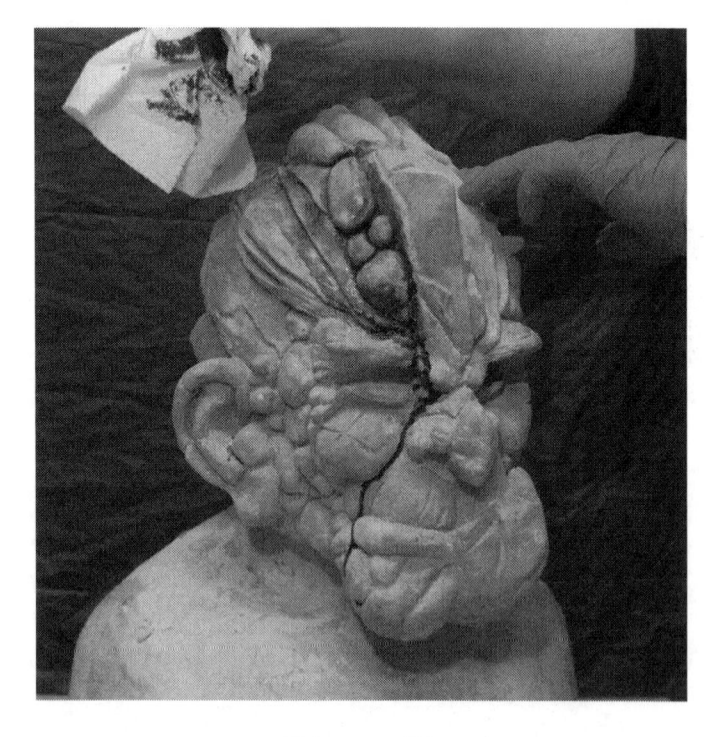

Diagram 72

Latex Mask Making

I take great care to dab off the paint—never wipe. Wiping removes too much paint and disturbs the look that the washes create. After the first wash I put the mask on a human analog armature to dry before adding another.

There is a lot of waiting involved, I know. It helps when you are painting multiple masks, props, or creatures. By the time you finish applying the first wash to the last mask, the first mask in the line is dry and you can move to the second wash. I understand that you only have one mask, and waiting for things to dry is probably killing you. It is important, though. You never want to rush it. But if you brought a fan in to speed things up, it wouldn't be the worst thing. It speeds up the drying process just enough. You don't want to go over board and use compressed air. It makes a mess.

When I'm done with washes and everything has dried, I use my finer paint brush and sponges and even my fingers to finish the painting. It sounds odd, I know. I figured you might not have access to an airbrush, and many of the workshops I teach my students don't either. I wanted to demonstrate how you can still get a great professional look without using an airbrush. Don't believe me? Below is a photograph of a bigfoot I created using nothing more than the techniques I am describing here. I managed to break my airbrush and didn't have time to order another. This critter was shipping in two days. I wasn't worried because I hadn't always had an airbrush to lean on. I knew I could kick out an amazing paint job without it. So, trust in Russ.

Russ Adams

Diagram 73

I apologize that I can't show you my references, but they are copyrighted materials, so for that reason I must keep them out of sight or blurred out. Taking a look at my references, I have one in particular, a gargoyle, that has some serious water stains on it. So I am going to play that up on my creature. I like the idea that guy has been rained on regularly over the years. Like a gargoyle, perhaps my rock creature is a sentry watching over a hidden kingdom.

Latex Mask Making

He doesn't move until danger finds the people he must protect. So I am going to punch up the water stains on the rock and mineral deposits. That means a darker wash and leaving it to dry a bit longer before dabbing off the remainder with a sponge.

Russ Adams

Fluid Stains

I have always found that the best way to mimic a fluid mark is to use thin paint. I just let an excess build up until the paint runs. I like the result.

I am deliberately putting too much paint in the ear canals and then coaxing it to run out, after which gravity deserves all the credit. You don't want the runoff to look perfect. Water is somewhat unpredictable as it scurries down a surface as it sees fit. Don't believe me, watch the water run down your skin the next time you get into the shower. It often changes direction, and in some very odd ways.

Sometime the runoff is too dark or thick. When this happens, I give the paint a second or two to stain the surface, and then chase it with a sponge…dabbing at it rather than wiping.

I use the same method with respect to eye sockets, mouth, and nostrils. These areas are a likely spot for the moisture to have accumulated and stained the rock before it ran off the face like river tributaries.

Latex Mask Making

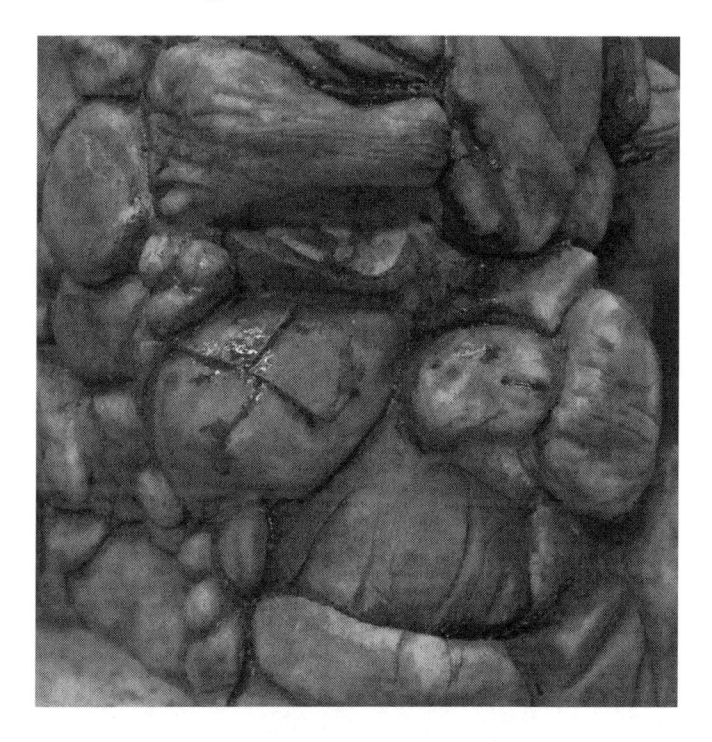

Diagram 74

Speckling

After each color is applied, I dip an old toothbrush into the wash. I knock off a bit of the excess, point it at the head, and gently flick a spray of droplets at the surface of the head. I will do this all the way around the mask.

On occasion there will be a large spot on the surface that doesn't look right. While it's still wet, I will knock it down with my fingertip. Just tap it down. The color will remain but will be more diffused. The flicking of colors adds a blotchy look, and simulates mineral deposits that might have been trapped during the formation of the rock in the Earth's mantle.

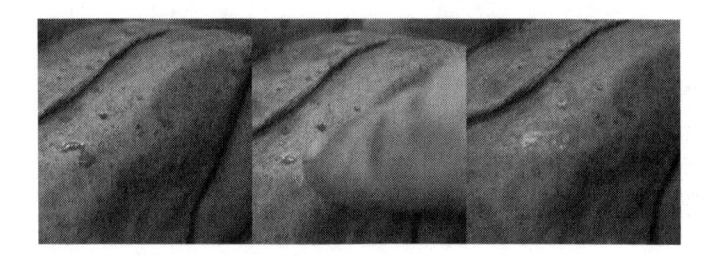

Diagram 75

I will also shade the deeper pockets of the face, eye orbits, inner ear, nose, and mouth with a darker grey. I might even chase it with some blue/black.

Each color I add will be followed by a flicking of that same color on the mask in the same way described earlier. There may be more of one color and less of another, but the process will continue until I am done painting.

Latex Mask Making

Highlights & Shadows

I want to hit the highlights and the shadows next. I am going to start with the highlights. This might sound silly to some, but there may be some people who don't know where to put the highlights. It's not always as simple as the brightening the high points. Here is a simple test to show you where to highlight your creature. Set the mask on the floor. Look straight down at it. You see the tips of the ears, crown of the head, brows, bridge of the nose, tops of the cheeks, upper lip, etc.

I want my highlights to look natural, so I am going to stagger them. I mix up a color that is a couple shades brighter than what is already there. This isn't a wash, but will be a bit watered down. I don't want a glob of dry paint on my mask. Using a torn piece of a sponge (material left over from a foam fabrication project) can become a paint brush of sorts. I will start with the brow. I always do…not sure why.

I will dab the paint on the area of the brow, one brow at a time. I say that because the paint tends to dry on one side while I am working on the other side. Once the paint is dabbed on the brow I will immediately knock it back with another piece of sponge, one that doesn't have paint on it.

Why a sponge with a rough edge? The rough edge is imperfect. I don't want there to be a solid area of paint. I want it to mottle. The subtle and rough torn edge adds an uneven and chaotic distribution of paint to the area of focus. I like that it does this because uniformity, in the case of my character, is not ideal.

Diagram 76

I will repeat this process in all the areas I mentioned, then move to a slightly brighter version of the same colors. Three colors, each a couple shades brighter than the last, should do the trick. But you should do more or less depending on what you want from your creature. Again, each of these colors will be flicked onto the mask in the same speckling method as was done with the washes.

Now the darker areas, the shadows. If you aren't sure where these areas are, simply turn the mask upside down and look straight down on it. The areas under the chin, jaw line, backs of the ear lobes, under the nose, under the brow, recesses of the eyes, etc. are the shadows.

The shadows are really a repeat of the highlights only with a darker paint. My plan is to employ the same process using the sponges. Don't go crazy with this. I am only going to use two colors and blend it out. For instance, I will start with the area below the chin. The plan is to add paint to the wider

Latex Mask Making

portion of the chin toward the jawline, then knock it back with the sponge. When I come back to this area with the second color, I will focus more in the center of the chin, and not in those border areas.

Russ Adams

Adornments

Once the painting is finished, it's time for facial adornment, like those lichens I talked about. Hell, it might even be cool to add tribal face paintings and duplicate their patterns on my mask. A rock creature is imposing enough, so I am not doing this for the scary factor. Instead, I am going to use it to soften this fella up.

I have decided he will use the tribal face painting to fit in with the human population he protects. Maybe he is self-conscious about being different. This helps him fit in.

The trick is not to be to exacting about the application of the tribal paint—the rougher you go, the better. I use sponges and chip brushes to apply colors like white/gray, blues, yellow ochre, and red. I often add powder to the color to make it appear as if it were a rustic grinding of pigments and water.

Latex Mask Making

Diagram 77

Russ Adams

MOSS

Another human-like factor is hair. Humanizing him a bit might be a good thing. Adding the illusion of facial hair might be a nice touch, but since rocks don't necessarily grow hair, I will use moss and plants to simulate it. You may even consider plant roots that scurry across your creature's face, like some hydroponic plant run amok.

Diagram 78

Latex Mask Making

WORKSHOP SUMMARY

Let's do a quick review of what we learned in this book. From making wooden and metal sculpting tools, to multiple methods of building your own armatures, you have learned that as a new artist you don't need to purchase expensive tools to create amazing pieces of work. Buying another artist's overpriced, low-quality tools isn't going to make you a better artist, just a poorer one. Making your own tools can be satisfying part of the process and it saves you money while making use of scrap materials that would otherwise end up in a landfill.

Russ Adams

You've learned how to build up an armature with clay to compensate for latex shrinkage, and the three basic, yet important steps to sculpting—blocking, rough detail, and fine detailing. These steps will slow you down. It will also prevent you from repeating your efforts and from prematurely creating detail that might later be destroyed. Follow these steps each time you sculpt and you will do fine.

We discussed sealing your sculpture and the sometimes terrifying prospect of molding it. My method isn't the only way to build a successful mold for your sculpture, but it's a tried and true process that has served me well for two decades. That said, I encourage you to watch other artists, learn from other tutorials. There is always a better way to do things. Take what you can from each method you learn and build on it. Until then, you have my method and a helpful checklist at the end of the book to guide you.

You learned how to demold a sculpture. Not an easy task the first few times you do it. Just remember to be patient and methodical about the process. If you are frustrated during a demold because something isn't separating properly, step away and come back to it later.

We also talked about mold straps and prepping a mold for casting. We talked about the casting process itself and how to demold a latex pull. This is probably the easiest part of the entire process. It's certainly not the most glamorous. There is nothing better than seeing that new latex mask pop out of a mold. A clean pull with infinite possibilities.

I talked about the cleaning and seaming process and how you can correct any mishaps that can occur. From horrid air bubble attacks to flashing mishaps, you now know how to deal with just about anything a bad casting day can throw at you.

Latex Mask Making

You learned that you don't need an airbrush to creature a professional paint job on your masks. Washes can be the name of the game. And who knew you could get a couple more uses out of those old sponges and upholstery foam? Oh, and good news for your kids. Finger painting can be a life skill.

Finally, you learned that painting isn't always enough to bring a mask to life. Sometimes it takes moss and twine, maybe some wooden beads to finish it off.

Mostly, I hope you gained the confidence to do this on your own—to take what I have taught you and put it to use. The biggest fear most people face coming into a project like this is the unknown. That's no longer the case for you. You know where to begin. You will become a good sculptor. You how to make this affordable. And you now know what to do if you screw up. So, get to work.

Russ Adams

Latex Mask Making

MOLD MAKING CHECKLIST

(Add notes you feel are important for you to remember.)

Do you have all your molding materials on hand ready?
___10-25 lbs of UltraCal 30 Plaster
___A Yard of Burlap Cut into 3"x3" squares
___Petroleum Jelly (release agent)
___A couple chip brushes
___A Disposable Cup for Water
___Mixing Sticks
___Dust Mask or Respirator
___Latex Gloves
___Black Marker
___2x4 Scraps
___WED Clay (For the mold process)
___Mixing Bowl
___Clear Matte Spray Paint

Have you sealed your sculpture with matte spray paint?

Building the case line
___Drawing a dotted dividing line with marker
___Pillow of clay covered with a sheet of plastic
___Gently lay sculpture back. Head resting face up and on the clay pillow.
___2x4 in place and secured with hot glued
___Use clay to build up to your dotted line DON'T TOUCH SCULPTURE
___Smooth the clay case line
___Now the clay case line should seamlessly meet the sculpture
___Retaining Wall
___Make registration marks and place them against the retaining wall
___Seal the clay with clear matte spray.

Inspect areas for undercut hazards.
___Neck
___Ears
___Ear Trench

Plaster Layer 1: The First Splash Coat
___Work out air bubbles
___Clean your brush. DON'T LEAVE IN WATER

Plaster Layer 2: The Second Splash Coat
___Work out air bubbles
___Clean your brush. DON'T LEAVE IN WATER

Plaster Layer 3: The Insurance Layer
___Lay burlap down on case line first
___Overlap burlap
___Work from case line up to the face of the sculpture.
___Work out air bubbles.
___Smoothen surface with a brush
___ Clean your brush. DON'T LEAVE IN WATER

Plaster Layer 4: The Protective Layer
___Thicker mix. Playdough
___Watch air bubbles.
___Spread this layer evenly across the surface
___Use brush to smooth surface
___ Clean your brush. DON'T LEAVE IN WATER

Name and Date on Side One

Prepping for Side Two
___Set sculpture upright
___Gently remove 2x4s (Break Hot Glue Bond with Rubbing Alcohol)
___Remove the Clay Build-up
___Remove Clay Wall
___Set Sculpture face down on work surface
___2x4s or clay to stabilize any wobbling
___Build side 2's retaining wall
___Cut and add pry marks and place them against the retaining wall.
___Petroleum Jelly coat on all plaster surfaces. CASE LINE NOT THE SCULPTURE

Repeat above steps from PLASTER LAYER 1

Latex Mask Making

Additional Information

You can find out more about Russ Adams's work at the following URLs;
Author Page (including appearances): www.russadams.me
Contact info@russadams.com
Professional Page: www.escapedesignfx.com
Contact admin@escapedesignfx.com

Follow this author on social media
Facebook www.facebook.com/escape.design,
INSTAGRAM @AdamsRuss,
TWITTER @EscapeDesign,
YouTube EscapeDesignFX

Russ Adams

Latex Mask Making

MANY MORE WORKSHOPS

TO COME

www.russadams.me

Russ Adams

PROJECT NOTES

PROJECT NOTES

Made in the USA
Columbia, SC
18 July 2017